INSPIRATIONAL MESSAGES WITH GRACE TO RESTORE

BOOK 2

ANITA HACKLEY LAMBERT

Copyright © 2024 Anita Hackley Lambert

All rights reserved.

No portion of this book may be reproduced or transmitted in any means, electronic or mechanical, including photocopying, recording, or by any information storage and retrieval system without written permission from the publisher or author. However, reviewers may quote brief passages as per U.S. Copyright Laws. This publication is designed to provide accurate and authoritative information regarding the subject matter covered. The publisher and author make no representations concerning the accuracy or completeness of the book's contents.

All Scripture is taken from the King James Bible.

Cover Designed by: Ashish Joshi

Library of Congress Cataloging-in-Publication Data is available.

Names: Lambert, Hackley, Anita, author.

Names: Lambert

TITLE: Soul Stirrings

Other titles: Soul Stirrings, Book 2

Description: Inspirational Devotional| HLE Publishing Company / Fort Washington

Identifiers: LCCN 2024921885 |ISBN 9798991483131 (paperback)|

ISBN 979-8-9914831-4-8 (eBook)|

ISBN 979-8-9914831-5-5 (hardcover)

LC record available at https://lccn.loc.gov/2024921885

ISBN 979-8-9914831-3-1

Order copies: Amazon.com and other online retailers.
Order Signature or Bulk Copies from the author:
AHackleyLambert@gmail.com

DEDICATION

This book is dedicated to you, my readers. I am boundless in gratitude and deeply appreciate your presence on this journey. You are the heart and soul of these pages, the reason for every word written and every message shared.

In your hands, you hold more than a book; you have a beacon of hope, a sanctuary of solace, and a reservoir of divine wisdom. My sincerest wish is that within these pages, you find the comfort you seek, the guidance you crave, and the inspiration you need to navigate life's challenges with courage and grace.

May the words herein remind you of your inherent worth, limitless potential, and divine connection to Jehovah God. May they uplift your spirit, soothe your soul, and ignite a flame of hope that burns brightly within you, even in the darkest times. And, thank you for entrusting me with your hearts and minds. It is an honor and a privilege to walk this journey with you, and I am deeply grateful for the opportunity to share these soul stirrings with you.

With love and blessings,
Anita Hackley Lambert, May 13, 2024

ACKNOWLEDGMENTS

First and foremost, writing "Soul Stirrings: Inspirational Messages Through Revelation " has been a transformative experience, deeply enriched by the presence, guidance, and inspiration of the Holy Spirit speaking into my heart.

Secondly, my heartfelt support also came from numerous extraordinary individuals. Their wisdom, encouragement, and faith have been the bedrock upon which this work has been built, and I acknowledge their contributions with immense gratitude.

My deepest gratitude goes to Pastor Angelo O. Jones of Heaven's Best Healing & Deliverance Church and my spiritual leader and teacher. Pastor Jones, your deep wisdom and spiritual insight have been a guiding light in my life and on this writing journey. Your teachings have enriched my understanding and stirred my soul, igniting a passion for spiritual growth and a deeper connection with God. Your unwavering support, encouragement, and countless hours of supernatural teachings have been instrumental in creating this book. Thank you for being dedicated to nurturing my spiritual journey and being a beacon of faith and wisdom.

To Minister Laurent Henderson, a walking testament to the Bible, your life and ministry are examples of faith in action. Your embodiment of the Scriptures in your daily walk has been a remarkable source of inspiration. Your depth of biblical knowledge encouraged me to infuse a solid foundation of scriptural truth. Your ability to tangibly and powerfully bring the Word of God to life has been a cornerstone of this work. Thank you for being a constant reminder of the power and beauty of a life rooted in the Word of God.

I am grateful to Pastor Rusty Hughes of Orchard Christian Center in Ballard, West Virginia. Your inspiring sermons and biblical messages have provided remarkable motivation and guidance. Your dedication to preaching the gospel and ability to make biblical principles relatable and applicable to everyday life have been invaluable. I appreciate your commitment to spreading God's word and the wisdom you have imparted through your sermons.

I am awestruck with overwhelming gratitude to my Pastor Fred and his wife and Co-Pastor, Debbie Ward of the Peterstown Church of God of Prophecy. Your spiritual influence has left an indelible mark on my heart for this portion of my journey. Your passionate and zealous commitment to spreading the gospel and unwavering faith have been sources of great inspiration. Your combined support is invaluable, providing wisdom, guidance, and support that has brought me to this point. Your prayers, encouragement, and steadfast faith have been pillars of strength, and I am deeply thankful for your presence in my life. To my family, your love and support have been the foundation for this work. Your faith in me, constant encouragement, and unwavering belief in this endeavor have been my bedrock. Each of you has played a crucial role in completing this book, offering love, patience, and support that have sustained me throughout this journey. I am immensely grateful for your presence in my life and the immeasurable ways you have contributed to this work.

I extend my heartfelt gratitude to my editor, Mike Valentino, whose exceptional dedication and meticulous attention have been pivotal in readying my book for publication. His insightful critiques and guidance have transformed my manuscript into a polished and compelling narrative. Mike's unwavering commitment to excellence, coupled with his passion for the Word of God and the written word, has elevated the quality of this work to new heights. His tireless efforts and invaluable contributions have been indispensable. I am deeply thankful for his steadfast support throughout this journey.

I cannot omit the host of Holy Spirit-filled fire carriers-- you know who you are. Each of you has walked this journey with me; your prayers, support, and spiritual hunger have ignited a passion within me that has fueled this work. Your friendship and unwavering faith, dedication to the work of the Holy Spirit, and fervent intercession have been a source of immense strength and inspiration. Thank you for your zeal and support and for being vessels of God's love and power. Your contributions are invaluable. I am deeply honored and humbled by your presence in my life.

This book is a testament to these remarkable individuals' collective influence and unwavering support. Their contributions have been instrumental in shaping this work, and I am eternally grateful for their roles in my journey. Please accept my heartfelt thanks and endless gratitude.

All scripture is given by inspiration of God, and is profitable for doctrine, for reproof, for correction, for instruction in righteousness: That the man of God may be perfect, thoroughly furnished unto all good works.
2 Timothy 3:16-17 (KJV)

CONTENTS

Preface i
Foreword iv
NO GREATER LOVE 1
IN GOD'S TIMING 33
CHANGE ON PURPOSE 54
RUN TO GOD 80
STAY HUNGRY FOR GOD 97
HIS WILL NOT YOURS 124
GOD ON YOU SIDE 147
A GUARDED HEART 169
A DARK PAST IS PAST 189
VESSEL OF HONOR 208
LOVE OF THE FATHER AND THE SON 219
KNOW WHO YOU ARE FOLLOWING 233
INSPIRE TO BE AN INSPIRATION 240
WHEN FAITH AND FEAR COLLIDE 246
LIMITLESS CHARITY 256

CONTENTS

SUCCESS IN CHARITY 263

MIRACLES 271

ENUMERABLE BLESSINGS 284

Epilogue 293

PREFACE

In the course of life, we all encounter moments when our spirits need renewal, when the weight of life's trials feels overwhelming. *"Soul Stirrings: Inspirational Messages with Grace to Restore"* is a beacon of hope and healing, offering divine inspiration for those seeking restoration, renewal, and a deeper connection to God's grace.

As you open the pages of *Soul Stirrings*, you enter a sacred space where God's transformative power is at work, ready to heal and restore. Each chapter is thoughtfully crafted to awaken the depths of your soul, infusing your life with purpose and guiding you toward the abundant blessings that flow from trusting in God's love and grace. Grounded in the eternal truths of scripture, this book is designed to inspire, uplift, and empower you to experience God's grace in a way that leads to restoration and spiritual renewal.

Within these pages, you will find reflections that speak to the heart of the human experience—acknowledging pain, struggles, and doubts, while also proclaiming the promise

PREFACE

of divine restoration through God's unshakable love. The message is clear: no matter what you face, God's grace is sufficient, and His restoration is boundless.

As you journey through the chapters of *Soul Stirrings*, may you find strength in knowing that you are never alone. God's presence is with you, guiding, healing, and restoring every broken part of your soul. May these words serve as a balm to your heart, igniting hope and stirring a deep faith that will empower you to rise above life's challenges. In the restoration that comes from God's grace, you will find the courage to persevere, the wisdom to trust, and the peace that only He can provide.

Let this journey be a reminder that through His grace, we are continually renewed, and with every step, we are being shaped into the person He has called us to be. May *Soul Stirrings* be an invitation to experience God's love and restoration in profound, life-changing ways.

FOREWORD

by Debbie Ward
Co-Pastor, Peterstown Church of God of Prophecy

When Anita and I met many years ago, our kindred spirits connected instantly—a spiritual and deeply resonant bond. Serving the Lord alongside her with her unwavering devotion to the vivid stirrings of her spirit has deeply moved me. Her dedication is unmistakable and shines through each page of this remarkable work, Soul Stirrings: Inspirational Messages Through Revelations. This book overflows with divine insight, offering a path toward spiritual awakening and illumination.

Anita's life has borne abundant fruit because she places her trust and obedience in a power higher than herself. Her legacy of living by a Higher Power leaves a trail of steady footprints, inviting us to follow her example.

FOREWORD

Life is a magnitude of choices, each shaping our journey toward discovering God's purpose. In Soul Stirrings, Anita speaks to the full depth of human experience, offering wisdom and empathy for our challenges. As you turn these pages, may you find comfort in God's unwavering promises and the assurance that He will never leave nor forsake us.

With heartfelt blessings,
Debbie Ward

""For by grace are ye saved through faith; and that not of yourselves: it is the gift of God: Not of works, lest any man should boast."
Ephesians 2:8-9, KJV

(Poem Scripture Reference)

GRACE TO RESTORE

(A Poem)

By Anita Hackley Lambert - September 15, 2024

When weary hearts have fallen low,
And hope seems dim and far,
God's grace, a river pure and bright,
Shines like a steadfast star.

Through storm and shadow, deep despair,
Where broken spirits weep,
His grace, a light that never fades,
Awakens from the sleep.

In moments where our strength gives way,
And fear begins to rise,
Grace whispers softly through the dark,
A balm for weary eyes.

It mends the soul that's torn with grief,
Restores what time had stolen,
A hand that lifts us from the dust,
And makes our hearts unbroken.

Through valleys deep, through darkest nights,
When hope is hard to find,
Grace leads us on, a steady flame,
Enlightening the mind.

GRACE TO RESTORE

In every trial, in every test,
When sorrow shakes our ground,
Grace steps in like a rushing tide,
To heal what's been unbound.

It calms the storm within the heart,
And turns the tears to peace,
Grace, the force that lifts us up,
And grants the soul release.

No wound too deep, no scar too great,
For God's love to restore,
In Him, the broken find their place,
And rise to live once more.

For in the arms of Heaven's light,
Our spirits find their wings,
Grace, the gift that mends the soul,
And to the broken sings.

When life feels lost, when dreams decay,
And darkness blinds the way,
Remember grace will find you still,
And guide you to the day.

God's mercy, vast as oceans deep,
Will carry you ashore,
And in His arms, we stand renewed,
Restored and whole once more.

CHAPTER 1

NO GREATER LOVE

THE ULTIMATE SACRIFICE AND DIVINE LOVE

""Greater love hath no man than this, that a man lay down his life for his friends."
John 5:13, KJV

GRATITUDE SHOULD BE A constant in our lives, yet we often fall into the "self-syndrome." As we reflect on God's infinite love for us, may this message, inspired by the Holy Spirit, serve as a reminder of that love.

We are fearfully and wonderfully made, dearly loved, and precious in the Lord's eyes. The psalmist captures this beautifully in Psalm 139:14 (KJV): "I will praise thee; for I am fearfully and wonderfully made: marvelous are thy works; and that my soul knoweth right well." God's love is steadfast and enduring. 1 John 3:1 (KJV) proclaims, "Behold, what manner of love the Father hath bestowed upon us, that we should be called the sons of God."

Let us appreciate the vastness of God's love. It transcends our understanding and meets us where we are, willing to sacrifice everything for our redemption. John 3:16 (KJV) affirms, "For God so loved the world, that he gave his only begotten Son, that whosoever believeth in him should not perish, but have everlasting life."

God's love is the foundation of our faith and identity as His children. It calls us to live with gratitude, to love others as He loves us, and to reflect His light in a world that desperately needs it. As we reflect on this love, let us be reminded of our immense value and worth. We are His beloved, created with purpose and destined for greatness in His Kingdom.

The Call to Live Out God's Love

As we delve into the Scriptures, we see the many facets of God's love and what it means for us as His children. May this message inspire us to move beyond self-centeredness and embrace a spirit of thanksgiving, recognizing the incredible love that God has poured out upon us.

Let us always commit to being thankful, allowing God's love to transform our hearts and minds. As we do, we will experience the fullness of joy and peace from knowing our Creator deeply loves us. May we always remember and celebrate the greatest love of all—the love of God for His children.

God's Steadfast and Unconditional Love

In moments of joy and times of trial, God's constant and unwavering love is our anchor. Deuteronomy 31:6 (KJV) reassures us, "Be strong and of a good courage, fear not, nor be afraid of them: for the Lord thy God, he it is that doth go with thee; he will not fail thee, nor forsake thee."

God's love is not conditional or fleeting. It is steadfast and eternal. Psalm 136 (KJV) repeats the phrase, "For his mercy endureth for ever," underscoring the enduring nature of His love and mercy. Each verse recounts God's mighty works and ends with a reminder of His everlasting love, encouraging us to reflect on the countless ways He has proven His faithfulness throughout history and in our lives.

In the New Testament, the assurance of God's unending love is further emphasized. Romans 8:38-39 (KJV) declares, "For I am persuaded, that neither death, nor life, nor angels, nor principalities, nor powers, nor things present, nor things to come, Nor height, nor depth, nor any other creature, shall be able to separate us from the love of God, which is in Christ Jesus our Lord." This powerful passage affirms that nothing in existence can sever us from God's love, a love that was most demonstrated through the sacrifice of Jesus Christ.

Understanding and believing in God's unchanging love transforms how we navigate life's challenges. It gives us the confidence to face difficulties with faith, knowing that we are never alone. God's love is a source of comfort and strength, guiding us through the darkest valleys and celebrating with us on the highest peaks.

Embracing the Fullness of God's Love

Moreover, God's perfect love casts out fear. 1 John 4:18 (KJV) tells us, "There is no fear in love; but perfect love casteth out fear: because fear hath torment. He that feareth is not made perfect in love." When we embrace the fullness of God's love, we find freedom from fear and anxiety. His love provides a safe haven where we can rest and find peace regardless of external circumstances.

As we journey through this chapter, let us deepen our understanding of God's perfect and enduring love. Let us hold firmly to the truth that His love is unfailing and everlasting. By doing so, we equip ourselves with the assurance and confidence needed to face life's uncertainties.

May this message encourage us to live with a heart full of gratitude and a spirit of deep faith. Let us continually remind ourselves and others of the truth that God's love never fails, and His presence is always with us. In every season and situation, we are enveloped by His perfect love, which endures forever.

God's love is holy, pure, and never limited. It is an indescribable love that will never change or fail. No one can fully comprehend the love of God and the magnitude of its power.

The Sacrificial Love of Jesus

God's love transcends human understanding. It is a love that goes beyond what we can imagine or articulate. Jeremiah 31:3 (KJV) declares, "The Lord hath appeared of old unto me, saying, Yea, I have loved thee with an everlasting love: therefore with lovingkindness have I drawn thee." This everlasting love draws us closer to Him, enveloping us in His grace and mercy.

The purity and holiness of God's love are unmatched. Unlike human love, which can be flawed and conditional, God's love is perfect and unchanging. It is a love that is not dependent on our actions or worthiness but is rooted in His very nature. 1 John 4:16 (KJV) reminds us, "And we have known and believed the love that God hath to us. God is love; and he that dwelleth in love dwelleth in God, and God in him." This truth highlights that God Himself is the essence of love, and His love for us is an extension of His Divine being.

God's love is also powerful beyond measure. Ephesians 3:18-19 (KJV) encourages us to "comprehend with all saints what is the breadth, and length, and depth, and height; And to know the love of Christ, which passeth knowledge, that ye might be filled with all the fulness of God." Though we may strive to grasp the enormity of His love, it surpasses all knowledge, filling us with the fullness of God.

This love is steadfast and eternal. It does not falter with our circumstances or change with time. Romans 8:38-39 (KJV) assures us, "For I am persuaded, that neither death, nor life, nor angels, nor principalities, nor powers, nor things present, nor things to come, Nor height, nor depth, nor any other creature, shall be able to separate us from the love of God, which is in Christ Jesus our Lord." Such assurance gives us the confidence to face any challenge, knowing that nothing can separate us from His love.

Living in the Light of God's Love

God's love is a refuge and a stronghold. It is a shelter that protects and comforts us in times of trouble. Psalm 36:7 (KJV) exclaims, "How excellent is thy lovingkindness, O God! therefore the children of men put their trust under the shadow of thy wings." Under the shadow of His wings, we find safety and peace, secure in knowing that His love surrounds us.

Let us continuously reflect on God's incredible, unfailing love. Let it inspire and encourage us, filling our hearts with gratitude and our spirits with joy. His love is a guiding light, a constant source of strength, and a reminder of our worth in His eyes.

May we live each day grounded in the assurance of God's holy, pure, and limitless love. Let us strive to share this love with others, reflecting God's heart in all we do. As we embrace the fullness of His love, we will find that it empowers us to live boldly, love deeply, and serve faithfully.

Let God's incomprehensible and unfailing love be our anchor and guide in every season of life. By dwelling in His love, we experience the true depth of His grace and the boundless nature of His mercy. Truly, there is no greater love than the love of God.

The Ultimate Sacrifice

The most amazing and greatest proof of God's love is when He sent His only Son, Jesus, to die on an old, rugged cross—the sacrifice of the Lamb of God for our sins—so we may be saved. Jesus suffered and died so we can live. He was resurrected and rose from the tomb. Jesus conquered death, hell, and the grave. He is alive! His love is alive! The nails didn't hold Jesus to the cross—it was His love for us.

The sacrificial love of Jesus is the cornerstone of our faith and the ultimate demonstration of God's boundless love for humanity. John 3:16 (KJV) declares, "For God so loved the world, that he gave his only begotten Son, that whosoever believeth in him should not perish, but have everlasting life." This verse encapsulates the magnitude of God's love, a love so great that He gave His Son to redeem us.

The suffering and death of Jesus on the cross were acts of love and sacrifice. Isaiah 53:5 (KJV) foretells, "But he was wounded for our transgressions, he was bruised for our iniquities: the chastisement of our peace was upon him; and with his stripes we are healed." Jesus endured unimaginable pain and suffering, taking upon Himself the punishment we deserved to bring us peace and healing.

The resurrection of Jesus is the triumphant victory over death and the grave. 1 Corinthians 15:55-57 (KJV) proclaims, "O death, where is thy sting? O grave, where is thy victory? The sting of death is sin; and the strength of sin is the law. But thanks be to God, which giveth us the victory through our Lord Jesus Christ." Through His resurrection, Jesus defeated the power of sin and death, offering us the hope of eternal life.

Jesus' love for us is active and enduring. As mentioned before, it was not the nails that held Him to the cross but His overwhelming love for us. Romans 5:8 (KJV) affirms, "But God commendeth his love toward us, in that, while we were yet sinners, Christ died for us." This unmerited love is the foundation of our salvation and the assurance of our relationship with God.

The resurrection is not just a historical event but a present reality. Jesus' love is alive, working in and through us today. This love empowers us to live boldly, love deeply, and serve faithfully. Galatians 2:20 (KJV) reminds us, "I am crucified with Christ: nevertheless I live; yet not I, but Christ liveth in me: and the life which I now live in the flesh

I live by the faith of the Son of God, who loved me and gave himself for me."

Reflecting on Jesus' Sacrifice

As we continue this chapter, let us reflect on Jesus' sacrifice and resurrection victory. Let this truth fill our hearts with gratitude and inspire us to live lives that honor His sacrifice. His love is the driving force behind our faith and the beacon that guides our actions.

May we embrace the reality of His living love and allow it to transform us. Let us share this incredible love with others, reflecting the heart of God in all we do. In every challenge and triumph, let the love of Jesus be our strength and our song, a testament to the greatest love the world has ever known.

In every moment, let us remember that we are loved with everlasting love, proven by the sacrifice of Jesus Christ. This love is our hope, our joy, and our life. Truly, there is no greater love than the love of God, made manifest in His Son, our Savior.

Embracing God's Forgiveness

It is an overwhelming thought that the Creator of heaven and earth loves me—loves you! These are the most powerful, life-changing words: "God loves you!" His love is so forgiving, especially when we are not so lovable when we grieve the Lord and the Holy Spirit. He loves us anyway. And because of what Jesus did at Calvary, God is faithful in forgiving us when we have done wrong and ask for forgiveness.

God's love is steadfast and unchanging, even when we fall short. 1 John 1:9 (KJV) promises, "If we confess our sins, he is faithful and just to forgive us our sins, and to cleanse us from all unrighteousness." This assurance is a testament to God's unwavering commitment to us. Despite our shortcomings, His love remains constant, inviting us to return to Him with a repentant heart.

The greatness of God's love is most evident in His willingness to forgive. Romans 5:8 (KJV) declares, "But God commendeth his love toward us, in that, while we were yet sinners, Christ died for us." Even in our sinfulness, God's love reaches out to us, offering redemption and restoration through the sacrifice of Jesus. This love is not dependent on our actions but reflects His perfect nature.

When we feel unworthy or overwhelmed by our mistakes, we can take comfort in knowing that God's love is greater than our failures. Psalm 103:12 (KJV) reassures us, "As far as the east is from the west, so far hath he removed our transgressions from us." This truth emphasizes the completeness of God's forgiveness and the boundless nature of His love.

God's love never gives up on us. Lamentations 3:22-23 (KJV) reminds us, "It is of the Lord's mercies that we are not consumed, because his compassions fail not. They are new every morning: great is thy faithfulness." Every day is a new opportunity to experience His mercy and grace, a testament to His enduring faithfulness.

As we reflect on the greatness of God's love, let us cultivate a spirit of thankfulness. His love is a gift that transforms our lives, offering hope and healing. When we recognize the depth of His love, our hearts are filled with gratitude, and we are inspired to live in a way that honors Him.

May we never take for granted God's overwhelming love. Let us be continually thankful for His everlasting love, which prevails despite our flaws and failures. This love is the foundation of our faith and the source of our strength.

God's Infinite Love

In every moment, let us remember that we are deeply loved by the Creator of the universe. His love forgives, restores, and renews. As we embrace this truth, we are empowered to live with joy and purpose, sharing the message of God's incredible love with others.

Truly, there is no greater love than the love of God, demonstrated through Jesus' sacrifice and the enduring presence of the Holy Spirit. Let this love be our guiding light, source of hope, and reason for thanksgiving. May we always be mindful of His unchanging love, and may it inspire us to love others as He has loved us.

If we can envision and multiply the most all-consuming love by infinity, that's the measure of God's love for us! "Give thanks—praise the God of heaven—for His steadfast love and mercy endure forever!" We are an imperfect people, but God loves us perfectly. He loves us for who we are. He says in His Word, "Come as you are." God only wants our praises and love in return.

The magnitude of God's love is beyond human comprehension. Ephesians 3:18-19 (KJV) encourages us to "comprehend with all saints what is the breadth, and length, and depth, and height; And to know the love of Christ, which passeth knowledge, that ye might be filled with all the fulness of God." His love surpasses our understanding, embracing us fully and completely.

God's love is unwavering and eternal. Psalm 136:26 (KJV) proclaims, "O give thanks unto the God of heaven: for his mercy endureth forever." His mercy and love are unending, inviting us to respond with gratitude and praise.

Despite our imperfections, God's love for us remains perfect, never wavering, never diminishing.

God loves us for who we are. He calls us to come to Him just as we are, without pretense or reservation. Matthew 11:28 (KJV) offers this invitation: "Come unto me, all ye that labour and are heavy laden, and I will give you rest." In our brokenness and imperfection, He welcomes us with open arms, offering rest and restoration. The Lord desires our praise and love in return. Psalm 100:4 (KJV) instructs us, "Enter into his gates with thanksgiving, and into his courts with praise: be thankful unto him, and bless his name." Our response to His infinite love should be gratitude and worship, acknowledging His goodness and mercy.

Living a Life of Gratitude

As we meditate on God's perfect love, let it transform our hearts and minds. This immeasurable and unconditional love should inspire us to live lives of thanksgiving and praise. In every circumstance, remember to thank the God of heaven, for His steadfast love endures forever.

May we embrace the reality of God's infinite love and let it guide our actions and attitudes. Let us love others as He has loved us, reflecting His grace and compassion in a world that desperately needs it. By living in the light of His love, we become beacons of hope and vessels of His mercy.

Let us be mindful of God's perfect love for us in every moment. This love does not depend on our perfection but is rooted in His unchanging nature. This love invites us to come as we are, to rest in His presence, and to respond with heartfelt praise and thanksgiving.

Truly, there is no greater love than the love of God, encompassing us in His infinite grace and mercy. Let us thank and praise the God of heaven, for His steadfast love and mercy endure forever. As we dwell in His love, may we be inspired to live lives that honor Him, filled with gratitude, joy, and a deep sense of His everlasting presence?

God's Unconditional Love

The remarkable thing about God's love is that it is not earned or merited. As humans—as His creation, as His children—we can do nothing to increase His love for us, nor can we do anything to lessen His love for us.

God's love is a gift freely given without conditions or prerequisites. Romans 5:8 (KJV) declares, "But God commendeth his love toward us, in that, while we were yet sinners, Christ died for us." This truth reminds us that God's love is not based on our worthiness but His grace and mercy. Even in our sinfulness, His love remains steadfast and unchanging.

Our human nature often leads us to believe that love must be earned through good deeds or lost through failures. However, God's love operates on a different plane. It is an unwavering, unconditional love that transcends our actions and circumstances. Ephesians 2:8-9 (KJV) states, "For by grace are ye saved through faith; and that not of yourselves: it is the gift of God: Not of works, lest any man should boast." Salvation and God's love are gifts, not rewards for our efforts. God's love for us is as constant as it is immeasurable. Jeremiah 31:3 (KJV) affirms, "The Lord hath appeared of old unto me, saying, Yea, I have loved thee with an everlasting love: therefore, with lovingkindness have I drawn thee." His everlasting love is a testament to His eternal commitment to us, drawing us to Him with tender mercy and grace.

There is no sin too great, no failure too intense, that can separate us from the love of God. Romans 8:38-39 (KJV) assures us, "For I am persuaded, that neither death, nor life, nor angels, nor principalities, nor powers, nor things present, nor things to come, Nor height, nor depth, nor any other creature, shall be able to separate us from the love of God, which is in Christ Jesus our Lord." This powerful declaration reinforces that God's love is all-encompassing and invincible.

Understanding that we cannot earn or diminish God's love should fill us with immense comfort and joy. It liberates us from the burden of striving for acceptance and frees us to embrace the fullness of His love. This understanding should also inspire us to love others with the same unconditional and unmerited love that God shows us.

1 John 4:19 (KJV) reminds us, "We love him, because he first loved us." Our love for God and others flows naturally from the love He pours into our hearts. As we grow in our awareness of His love, we are empowered to reflect that love in our relationships, actions, and daily lives. Let us rest in the assurance of God's steadfast love, knowing that it depends not on our performance but on His unchanging nature. May this truth inspire us to live with confidence and gratitude, secure in the knowing that we are deeply and eternally loved.

In every situation, let us hold fast to the reality of God's unearned, unmerited love. It transforms, heals, and sustains us, drawing us forever closer to Him. As we continue this chapter, we may be reminded of our Heavenly Father's boundless, unconditional love.

Truly, there is no greater love than the love of God, which is perfect, complete, and unfathomable. Let us rejoice in this love, sharing it freely with others and living in the light of His everlasting grace and mercy.

Reflecting God's Love

God's love for us is far deeper and stronger than ever imagined. His love is constant, abundant, and unwavering. The magnitude of His love is beyond our comprehension, enveloping us in grace and mercy at every moment. God's love is an astonishing mystery that we can begin to fathom. Ephesians 3:18-19 (KJV) encourages us to "comprehend with all saints what is the breadth, and length, and depth, and height; And to know the love of Christ, which passeth knowledge, that ye might be filled with all the fulness of God." This passage challenges us to grasp the vastness of Christ's love, a love that surpasses all understanding and fills us with the fullness of God.

God's Word calls us to respond to His love with our whole being. Matthew 22:37 (KJV) instructs us, "Thou shalt love the Lord thy God with all thy heart, and with all thy soul, and with all thy mind." This commandment calls us to immerse ourselves fully in God's love, allowing it to permeate every aspect of our lives.

Our love for God is a response to His overwhelming love for us. 1 John 4:19 (KJV) says, "We love him, because he first loved us." Our ability to love God and others flows from recognizing His immense love for us. As we understand His love, we are inspired to love Him with all our heart, soul, and mind.

Reflecting on God's deep and strong love for us should fill us with awe and gratitude. Love is not contingent on our actions but rooted in His unchanging nature. This love transforms us, calling us to live lives that honor and glorify Him.

As we explore the depths of God's love, let us open our hearts to receive and embrace it fully. May His love fill us with joy, peace, and a renewed sense of purpose. Let us strive to love the Lord our God with all our heart, soul, and mind, allowing His love to guide and direct our every step.

Truly, there is no greater love than the love of God. It is a love that is deeper and stronger than we can ever imagine, a love that is constant, abundant, and unwavering. Let us rejoice in this love, giving thanks to the God of heaven, for His steadfast love and mercy endure forever. As we dwell in His love, may we be inspired to share it with others, reflecting the heart of God in all that we do.

The Reality of God's Love

The reality of God's love surrounds us every day. God's love is revealed through His Son, Jesus Christ, and poured into us through the Holy Spirit. God's love compels us to love one another. We must know and experience God's love to be able to love one another—or ourselves—as we should.

The revelation of God's love through Jesus Christ is the cornerstone of our faith. John 3:16 (KJV) declares, "For God so loved the world, that he gave his only begotten Son, that whosoever believeth in him should not perish, but have everlasting life." This verse encapsulates the depth and breadth of God's love, demonstrated through the sacrifice of His Son. Jesus' life, death, and resurrection are the ultimate expressions of God's love for humanity.

God's love is poured into our hearts through the Holy Spirit. Romans 5:5 (KJV) assures us, "And hope maketh not ashamed; because the love of God is shed abroad in our hearts by the Holy Ghost which is given unto us." The Holy Spirit fills us with God's love, enabling us to experience it deeply and personally. This Divine love empowers us to live in a way that reflects God's character and grace.

God's love compels us to love one another. 1 John 4:11 (KJV) instructs us, "Beloved, if God so loved us, we ought also to love one another." This commandment highlights the transformative power of experiencing God's love. When we truly grasp the magnitude of His love for us, it naturally overflows into our relationships with others. We are called to love as He loves, with a selfless and sacrificial love.

To genuinely love one another and ourselves, we must first know and experience the love of God. Ephesians 3:17-19 (KJV) encourages us, "That Christ may dwell in your hearts by faith; that ye, being rooted and grounded in love, May be able to comprehend with all saints what is the breadth, and length, and depth, and height; And to know the love of Christ, which passeth knowledge, that ye might be filled with all the fulness of God." Being rooted and grounded in God's love transforms our hearts and minds, equipping us to live authentically and fully.

Reflecting on the reality of God's love should inspire us daily. His love is not a distant concept but a living and active force. It surrounds us, sustains us, and guides us. As we become more aware of His love, we are empowered to live out the greatest commandments: to love God with all our heart, soul, and mind and to love our neighbors as ourselves (Matthew 22:37-39 KJV).

Let us embrace the reality of God's love and allow it to transform us. As we do, we will find that our capacity to love others and ourselves grows exponentially. This love is not something we generate on our own but is a gift from God, poured into our hearts by the Holy Spirit. It compels us to act with compassion, kindness, and grace, reflecting the heart of God in all that we do.

The Power of God's Love

In every moment, let us be mindful of the truth that God loves us. This love is revealed through Jesus Christ, infused into us by the Holy Spirit, and compels us to love others. As we dwell in His love, may we be inspired to share it with the world, living out the reality of God's infinite and unchanging love.

Truly, there is no greater love than the love of God, a love that is revealed, poured out, and compelling. Let us rejoice in this love, giving thanks to the God of heaven, for His steadfast love and mercy endure forever.

God graciously bestows His grace and mercy daily, showcasing His unwavering love and favor. This Divine favor serves as our protection, a testament to the Lord's steadfast faithfulness. He honors our faithfulness and obedience to Him, recognizing our persistence in seeking

His presence. In return, He fortifies and shields us from the evil forces that threaten to harm us.

God's protection is likened to a shield, His wings providing a refuge in times of danger. He assures us through His Word that "No weapon that is formed against thee shall prosper" (Isaiah 54:17). This Divine assurance means that we need not fear destruction or harm, for He is our haven. His love, a source of immense joy, becomes our strength. As it is written, "The joy of the LORD is your strength" (Nehemiah 8:10). In times of peril and need, God is our ever-present help, steadfast refuge, and our place of safety.

He declares in His Word, "The LORD is faithful, who shall stablish you, and keep you from evil" (2 Thessalonians 3:3). This promise strengthens our resolve and emboldens our faith. God is our refuge and fortress, as the Psalmist proclaims, "The LORD is my rock, and my fortress, and my deliverer; my God, my strength, in whom I will trust; my buckler, and the horn of my salvation, and my high tower" (Psalm 18:2).

In moments of uncertainty and trouble, we find solace in knowing that "God is our refuge and strength, a very present help in trouble" (Psalm 46:1). His love envelops us, offering joy and strength, guiding us through life's challenges. This Divine protection and ceaseless love remind us that we are shielded, strengthened, and eternally secure with God on our side.

Love and Obedience

The message of God's love is boundlessly powerful—it's a gift. "For God so loved the world, that He gave His only begotten Son, that whosoever believeth in Him should not perish, but have everlasting life" (John 3:16). God loves us deeply and unconditionally. He desires that we love Him in return. This love extends beyond our relationship with Him; He commands us to love one another, as it is written, "Thou shalt love thy neighbour as thyself" (Matthew 22:39). God's ultimate desire is for us to be with Him in Heaven, basking in His eternal presence.

"It is not His will that any should perish, but that all should come to repentance" (2 Peter 3:9). God's heart yearns for everyone to turn to Him and receive His grace. He does not send people to Hell; our choices determine our eternal destiny. When we reject His love and grace, we separate ourselves from Him. Hell is a place for those who trespass against His Divine will, not because He desires it, but because of our decisions.

God's love calls us to a higher standard, urging us to embrace His gift of salvation. As the Scripture declares, "The Lord is not slack concerning His promise, as some men count slackness; but is longsuffering to us-ward, not willing that any should perish, but that all should come to repentance" (2 Peter 3:9). This love transforms and redeems, offering us the hope of eternal life. In accepting this gift, we align ourselves with His will, ensuring that we do not end up as trespassers in a place never intended for us. Let us choose wisely, embracing His love and sharing it with others so we may all rejoice in His heavenly kingdom.

By embracing God's love, we fulfill His greatest commandments. "And thou shalt love the Lord thy God with all thy heart, and with all thy soul, and with all thy mind, and with all thy strength: this is the first commandment. And the second is like this: Thou shalt love thy neighbour as thyself. There is none other commandment greater than these" (Mark 12:30-31). Let us live out these truths, reflecting God's love in our actions and choices and leading others to joy and peace in His Divine embrace.

True Faith in Action

True faith powerfully demonstrates our love for God and others. This faith is not merely a belief but a steadfast trust in God's love for us, regardless of our circumstances. As the Scripture declares, "Now faith is the substance of things hoped for, the evidence of things not seen"

(Hebrews 11:1). God's love serves as our safe harbor, offering refuge and comfort during trials.

When we fully submit to God and earnestly desire His love, we tap into a transformative power that heals all things and overcomes all evil. "For whatsoever is born of God overcometh the world: and this is the victory that overcometh the world, even our faith" (1 John 5:4). God's love provides safety and security, grounding us in truth and allowing us to understand deeper spiritual realities. "And ye shall know the truth, and the truth shall make you free" (John 8:32).

Through God's love, we experience the Divine power of the Holy Spirit. "But the Comforter, which is the Holy Ghost, whom the Father will send in my name, he shall teach you all things, and bring all things to your remembrance, whatsoever I have said unto you" (John 14:26). This Divine love is the only true source of happiness and peace we have. "And the peace of God, which passeth all understanding, shall keep your hearts and minds through Christ Jesus" (Philippians 4:7).

God's love is the core of our faith, enabling us to live in truth and experience the fullness of His Spirit. It is through this love that we find our ultimate joy and peace, as the Psalmist declares, "The Lord is my shepherd; I shall not want. He maketh me to lie down in green pastures: he leadeth me beside the still waters. He restoreth my soul" (Psalm 23:1-3).

Let us hold fast to this true faith, trusting in God's unending love and allowing it to guide our lives. By doing so, we embrace the true source of happiness and peace, living in the light of His eternal love. "For I am persuaded, that neither death, nor life, nor angels, nor principalities, nor powers, nor things present, nor things to come, nor height, nor depth, nor any other creature, shall be able to separate us from the love of God, which is in Christ Jesus our Lord" (Romans 8:38-39).

May our faith in God's love be unalterable as we seek to live out His commandments and share His love with the world. "And thou shalt love the Lord thy God with all thy heart, and with all thy soul, and with all thy mind, and with all thy strength: this is the first commandment. And the second is like-minded, namely this, Thou shalt love thy neighbour as thyself. There is none other commandment greater than these" (Mark 12:30-31).

By embracing God's love and reflecting it in our lives, we fulfill His greatest commandments and find true joy and peace. Let us live out these truths, confident in His love and guided by His Spirit, knowing that we are secure, strengthened, and eternally blessed in His love.

Spiritual Health and Love for God

This insight offers immense clarity: our spiritual health is directly proportionate to our love for God. Reflect deeply on this concept. Are we spiritually healthy and flourishing, or are we spiritually malnourished and ailing? We profess our love for God, but do our actions and daily lives bear witness to that love? This reflection is deeply personal—how exactly is our love for God measured?

Consider this assurance: God is far more faithful to us than we could ever be to Him. "It is of the LORD's mercies that we are not consumed, because his compassions fail not. They are new every morning: great is thy faithfulness" (Lamentations 3:22-23). God's unwavering faithfulness is a testament for us to emulate in our devotion and love for Him.

Our spiritual well-being hinges on our relationship with God. "Draw nigh to God, and he will draw nigh to you" (James 4:8). This Scripture emphasizes that our spiritual health and overall well-being are directly correlated with our earnest love and pursuit of Him.

We must evaluate our lives critically. Do our actions, choices, and daily routines reflect a deep and abiding love for God? "If ye love me, keep my commandments" (John 14:15). True love for God manifests in obedience and a lifestyle that honors Him. It requires us to live out our faith authentically, demonstrating our devotion through our deeds.

God's faithfulness is a cornerstone of our spiritual lives. "Know therefore that the LORD thy God, he is God, the faithful God, which keepeth covenant and mercy with them that love him and keep his commandments to a thousand generations" (Deuteronomy 7:9). His faithfulness reassures us and inspires us to reciprocate with genuine love and commitment.

Let us strive to align our spiritual health with our love for God. As we do, we honor Him and cultivate a vibrant, flourishing spiritual life. "But seek ye first the kingdom of God, and his righteousness; and all these things shall be added unto you" (Matthew 6:33). Prioritizing our love for God leads to spiritual prosperity and a deeper, more meaningful connection with Him.

May our lives reflect our true love for God, not just in words but every aspect of our being. Let us draw closer to Him, seek His guidance, and live in a way that testifies to our faith. "For in him we live, and move, and have our being" (Acts 17:28). In doing so, we will experience the fullness of His love and the richness of a spiritually healthy life.

A Life of Gratitude and Wonder

To experience God's true, enduring love, reflect on the privilege of being alive. Consider the miraculous abilities we possess: to breathe, think, enjoy life, and love God, family, and friends. This perspective transforms our daily existence into a symphony of gratitude and wonder.

Life itself is a testament to God's boundless love and mercy. "It is of the LORD's mercies that we are not consumed because his compassions fail not" (Lamentations 3:22). Every breath we take, every thought we ponder, and every joy we experience reminds us of His sustaining grace. The capacity to love and be loved is a Divine gift that connects us to God's eternal love.

We often overlook the simple blessings that surround us in our daily lives. The laughter of loved ones, warmth of friendship, and beauty of creation reflect God's love for us. "O give thanks unto the LORD; for he is good; for his mercy endureth forever" (1 Chronicles 16:34). By cultivating a heart of gratitude, we open ourselves to a deeper understanding and appreciation of God's enduring love.

Being thankful to the God of Heaven for His love transforms our perspective on life. "In everything give thanks: for this is the will of God in Christ Jesus concerning you" (1 Thessalonians 5:18). Gratitude shifts our focus from what we lack to the abundant blessings we receive daily. It fosters a spirit of joy and contentment rooted in the assurance of God's never-ending love.

Consider His sacrifice to truly grasp the magnitude of God's love. "But God commendeth his love toward us, in that, while we were yet sinners, Christ died for us" (Romans 5:8). This ultimate act of love and redemption underscores the depth of His commitment to us. Through this sacrificial love, we find the strength to love others and live a life of purpose and fulfillment.

In moments of reflection, let us remember the precious privilege of life and the endless love of our Creator. "Bless the LORD, O my soul, and forget not all his benefits" (Psalm 103:2). By acknowledging and embracing His love, we draw closer to Him, enriching our spiritual journey and fostering a deeper connection with those around us.

May we continually express our gratitude to God, recognizing His love in every aspect of our lives. "Praise ye the LORD. O give thanks unto the LORD; for he is good: for his mercy endureth forever" (Psalm 106:1). In doing so, we align our hearts with His Divine purpose, experiencing the fullness of His love and the joy that comes from living a life of gratitude and devotion.

Be blessed in the Lord always!

CHAPTER 2

IN GOD'S TIMING

THIS TOO SHALL PASS

""To everything there is a season, and a time to every purpose under the heaven." Ecclesiastes 3:1, KJV

IN MATTHEW 16:18, KJV the scripture declares "The gates of hell shall not prevail against it." This declaration reassures us of God's invincible strength and unwavering promise of protection. In our moments of deepest despair, when we feel overwhelmed and believe we cannot continue, God's power shines through our weaknesses. "My grace is sufficient for thee: for my strength is made perfect in weakness" (2 Corinthians 12:9). Through the Lord, our weakness transforms into strength, revealing a resilience we never even knew we had.

Life often appears unfair and filled with challenges and hardships. Take heart, for this too shall pass. As we navigate trials and struggles, we enter a period of significant learning and growth. God uses these times to fortify us, making us more resilient as the days pass. "And we know that all things work together for good to them that love God, to them who are the called according to his purpose" (Romans 8:28).

Resilience involves enduring and actively engaging with our God-given resources, strengths, and skills. The Holy Spirit equips us to overcome adversity and move forward in Jesus' name. "I can do all things through Christ which strengtheneth me" (Philippians 4:13). This inner reservoir of strength, a mental and spiritual wellspring, sustains us and keeps us from falling apart.

During our most challenging times, it is crucial to remember that God's timing is perfect. He knows our needs and strengthens us precisely when we need it most. As we endure and persevere, we are not merely surviving but growing, becoming more durable, and prepared for what lies ahead. "But they that wait upon the LORD shall renew their strength; they shall mount up with wings as eagles; they shall run, and not be weary; and they shall walk, and not faint" (Isaiah 40:31).

In every trial, never forget that God's power is at work within us, turning our weaknesses into strengths. The Lord magnifies our capacity for endurance and resilience. As we lean on His strength, we find the courage to keep going, knowing that every challenge we face is an opportunity for growth and transformation. "We are troubled on every side, yet not distressed; we are perplexed, but not in despair; persecuted, but not forsaken; cast down, but not destroyed" (2 Corinthians 4:8-9).

Let this chapter encourage you. No matter how difficult life may seem, know that this shall pass through God's timing and power. Embrace the journey, trust in His plan, and allow His strength to carry you through regardless of circumstances. "The LORD is my rock, and my fortress, and my deliverer; my God, my strength, in whom I will trust" (Psalm 18:2).

We can face adversity with faith in God's rock-solid promise and steadfast love, knowing His strength is perfect in our weakness. "For I know the thoughts that I think toward you, saith the LORD, thoughts of peace, and not of evil, to give you an expected end" (Jeremiah 29:11). Trust in His Divine timing, for He will guide us through every storm and lead us to a place of peace and strength.

Often, we do not realize our true strength until we have no choice but to be strong. It is in these moments of trial and suffering that our character is forged and refined. "Knowing this, that the trying of your faith worketh patience" (James 1:3). Through these experiences, we are empowered and equipped for greater things.

Our strength does not come from an absence of failures but from our perseverance through them. "But the God of all grace, who hath called us unto his eternal glory by Christ Jesus, after that ye have suffered a while, make you perfect, stablish, strengthen, settle you" (1 Peter 5:10). With the Holy Spirit as our power source, we become unstoppable, not because we do not face difficulties, but precisely because we continue moving forward despite them.

When the enemy attacks, we must hold fast. These moments are not just tests but elevations. "But they that wait upon the LORD shall renew their strength; they shall mount up with wings as eagles; they shall run, and not be weary; and they shall walk, and not faint" (Isaiah 40:31).

Each trial is an opportunity for growth, a chance to rise above our circumstances with renewed strength and courage.

Take heart and be strong, for this too shall pass. The challenges we face are temporary, but the strength and resilience we gain from them are eternal. "And let us not be weary in well doing: for in due season we shall reap, if we faint not" (Galatians 6:9). Every struggle is a stepping stone to greater faith and fortitude, building us up for the journey ahead.

In the face of adversity, remember that God is with us, guiding us and providing the strength we need to endure. "Fear thou not; for I am with thee: be not dismayed; for I am thy God: I will strengthen thee; yea, I will help thee; yea, I will uphold thee with the right hand of my righteousness" (Isaiah 41:10). With His help, we can overcome any obstacle and emerge stronger on the other side.

As we navigate life's trials, let us rely on our faith and trust God's timing. "For I reckon that the sufferings of this present time are not worthy of being compared with the glory which shall be revealed in us" (Romans 8:18). The difficulties we face today are shaping us for the future, preparing us for the blessings and glory God has in store.

In every challenge, find hope and encouragement in the knowledge that God is actively working in our lives. "And we know that all things work together for good to them that love God, to them who are the called according to his purpose" (Romans 8:28). Trust in His Divine plan and draw strength from His unfailing love and grace.

When life seems overwhelming, and we are tempted to give up, let us remember that God's power is made perfect in our weakness. "And he said unto me, My grace is sufficient for thee: for my strength is made perfect in weakness" (2 Corinthians 12:9). Through our trials, we are refined, strengthened, and prepared for the greater purposes He has for us.

Take courage and be strong, for this too shall pass. Let us continue to press forward with faith and determination, knowing that we are more than conquerors with God on our side. "Nay, in all these things we are more than conquerors through him that loved us" (Romans 8:37). In God's perfect timing, every trial will testify to His faithfulness and love.

God, in His infinite wisdom and compassionate authority, allows us to struggle even though His power could prevent it. This understanding reveals a truth: the benefit of our struggles far outweighs the comfort we might experience from immediate rescue. "And not only so, but we glory in tribulations also: knowing that tribulation worketh patience; and patience, experience; and experience, hope" (Romans 5:3-4). Through our trials, we develop patience, character, and hope, essential qualities that shape our spiritual journey.

God's wisdom in allowing us to face challenges highlights His desire to grow and strengthen our faith. "My grace is sufficient for thee: for my strength is made perfect in weakness" (2 Corinthians 12:9). In our weakest moments, His power is most evident, teaching us to rely on Him completely. This dependency fosters a deeper relationship with our Creator as we learn to trust His provision and guidance.

God wants us to depend on Him and Him alone. "Trust in the LORD with all thine heart; and lean not unto thine own understanding. In all thy ways acknowledge him, and he shall direct thy paths" (Proverbs 3:5-6). We find peace and strength that surpasses our understanding by surrendering our will and trusting in His plan.

The promise of God's healing power is a source of immense comfort and hope. "I have heard thy prayer, I have seen thy tears: behold, I will heal thee" (2 Kings 20:5). He sees our pain and cries, assuring us of His presence and willingness to heal our broken hearts. However, we must allow God to heal us fully. Opening our hearts to His healing touch prevents the destructive consequences of unresolved pain.

To experience true healing, we must surrender our burdens to God and trust His timing. "Casting all your care upon him; for he careth for you" (1 Peter 5:7). Holding onto pain and refusing to let God heal us only prolongs our suffering and hinders our spiritual growth. When we release our struggles into His capable hands, we invite His peace and restoration into our lives.

As we journey through life's challenges, let us remember that God's grace is all we need. His strength is perfected in our weakness, and His love is a constant source of comfort and encouragement. "The LORD is nigh unto them that are of a broken heart; and saveth such as be of a contrite spirit" (Psalm 34:18). Embrace His healing power, and trust that in His timing, every pain will pass, and every trial will lead to a testimony of His faithfulness.

By allowing God to heal our hearts, we open ourselves to the transformative power of His love. "He healeth the broken in heart, and bindeth up their wounds" (Psalm 147:3). This healing not only restores us but empowers us to move forward with renewed strength and purpose. Let us praise the sweet God of heaven for His grace, power, and unwavering love.

In every struggle, find hope in the knowledge that God is with us, working all things for our good. "And we know that all things work together for good to them that love God, to them who are the called according to his purpose" (Romans 8:28). Trust in His Divine plan, and take courage in the assurance that this too shall pass, bringing us closer to the fullness of His promises and the joy of His presence.

God is beyond error and perfect in all His ways. His sovereignty and mercy are infinite, guiding us through every aspect of our lives. "As for God, his way is perfect: the word of the LORD is tried: he is a buckler to all those that trust in him" (Psalm 18:30). We are called to humble ourselves before Him, conforming to His will rather than foolishly expecting Him to conform to ours. "Humble yourselves under the mighty hand of God, that he may exalt you in due time" (1 Peter 5:6).

God's favor envelops His children, offering protection and guidance. "For thou, LORD, wilt bless the righteous; with favour wilt thou compass him as with a shield" (Psalm 5:12). Even now, He is aligning circumstances for our ultimate good, orchestrating our lives with His perfect wisdom. Hallelujah!

In submission to God, we understand that our storms are temporary, but His blessings are eternal. "For our light affliction, which is but for a moment, worketh for us a far more exceeding and eternal weight of glory" (2 Corinthians 4:17). The challenges we face are indeed fleeting. Still, the rewards of our faith and obedience are everlasting. In life's storms, we must remind ourselves that God is in control and that He answers prayer. "The effectual fervent prayer of a righteous man availeth much" (James 5:16).

Embracing God's sovereignty allows us to face our struggles with confidence and hope. "And we know that all things work together for good to them that love God, to them who are the called according to his purpose" (Romans 8:28). By trusting in His Divine plan, we can find peace even in the most turbulent times, knowing that this too shall pass.

Let us continually submit our lives to God's perfect will, acknowledging His power and mercy. "Submit yourselves therefore to God. Resist the devil, and he will flee from you" (James 4:7). In doing so, we find strength and resilience and align ourselves with the blessings He has prepared for us.

As we bravely face life's challenges, let us focus on God's eternal promises. "For I know the thoughts that I think toward you, saith the LORD, thoughts of peace, and not of evil, to give you an expected end" (Jeremiah 29:11). His plans for us are filled with hope and a future. By trusting in His timing and purpose, we can endure our present trials with the assurance that brighter days are ahead.

In every storm, let us acknowledge that God's favor and blessings are upon us. "The LORD is my shepherd; I shall not want. He maketh me to lie down in green pastures: he leadeth me beside the still waters. He restoreth my soul: he leadeth me in the paths of righteousness for his name's sake" (Psalm 23:1-3). His provision and care are unending, guiding us through every challenge and leading us to peace and restoration.

As we continue this chapter in our lives, may we hold fast to our faith, submit to God's will, and trust His perfect plan. With God in control, every storm will pass, and we will emerge stronger, blessed, and more resilient, ready to experience the joy of the future He has lovingly prepared for us. "But they that wait upon the LORD shall renew their strength; they shall mount up with wings as eagles; they shall run, and not be weary; and they shall walk, and not faint" (Isaiah 40:31).

The Lord stands with us and gives us strength. "The LORD is my strength and my shield; my heart trusted in him, and I am helped" (Psalm 28:7). If God does not empty our cup of suffering or take it away, He provides ample grace, favor, and ability to bear it. "And he said unto me, My grace is sufficient for thee: for my strength is made perfect in weakness" (2 Corinthians 12:9). We must let go of the emotions and burdens that develop from the struggle and the test and grow from it.

Growth, resilience, and strength give us flexibility in mind and spirit, enabling us not to break under pressure. "But the God of all grace, who hath called us unto his eternal glory by Christ Jesus, after that ye have suffered a while, make you perfect, stablish, strengthen, settle you" (1 Peter 5:10). We learn to take what comes, knowing that each challenge is an opportunity for growth. We survive, trusting in God's provision and support.

When we fall, we get up and keep fighting to see another day, believing this will pass. "For a just man falleth seven times, and riseth up again" (Proverbs 24:16). Each time we rise, we demonstrate our faith in God's promises and His unfailing support.

In moments of trial, it is crucial to remember that God is with us, providing the strength we need to endure. "Fear thou not; for I am with thee: be not dismayed; for I am thy God: I will strengthen thee; yea, I will help thee; yea, I will uphold thee with the right hand of my righteousness" (Isaiah 41:10). His presence is a constant source of encouragement and empowerment.

As we navigate the storms of life, let us hold onto the assurance that God's grace is sufficient for every challenge. "Casting all your care upon him; for he careth for you" (1 Peter 5:7). By releasing our burdens to Him, we find the strength to persevere and the peace that surpasses all understanding.

Through every struggle, we are refined and strengthened. "But they that wait upon the LORD shall renew their strength; they shall mount up with wings as eagles; they shall run, and not be weary; and they shall walk, and not faint" (Isaiah 40:31). Our resilience is a testament to God's faithfulness and our trust in His perfect timing.

May we grow in faith, resilience, and strength, trusting that God's grace will carry us through every trial. "I can do all things through Christ which strengtheneth me" (Philippians 4:13). With God by our side, we can face any challenge, knowing that this too shall pass and brighter days are ahead.

God's Word reassures us, "My flesh and my heart faileth: but God is the strength of my heart, and my portion forever" (Psalm 73:26). In moments of weakness and despair, this truth provides comfort and hope. Even when our strength falters, God remains our eternal source of power and sustenance.

We must strive to be so deeply rooted and grounded in God that nothing and no one can disturb our peace. "That Christ may dwell in your hearts by faith; that ye, being rooted and grounded in love" (Ephesians 3:17). This deep connection with God fortifies our spirit, ensuring that we remain steadfast regardless of the storms we face.

Our peace comes from the unwavering knowledge that we can "hang on tight" because this, too, shall pass. "And the peace of God, which passeth all understanding, shall keep your hearts and minds through Christ Jesus" (Philippians 4:7). This Divine peace transcends our circumstances, providing us with a calm assurance that God is in control and that our trials are temporary.

In moments of trial, we must remind ourselves of God's promises. "He giveth power to the faint; and to them that have no might he increaseth strength" (Isaiah 40:29). His strength is made perfect in our weakness, and His presence is our constant support. We are encouraged to trust in His timing and plan, knowing He works all things together for our good.

As we face life's challenges, let us take solace in the hope God's word provides. "For whatsoever things were written aforetime were written for our learning, that we through patience and comfort of the Scriptures might have hope" (Romans 15:4). The Scriptures are a wellspring of encouragement, reminding us that God's promises are true and His love is everlasting.

May we draw near to God, finding our strength and peace in Him alone. "Draw nigh to God, and he will draw nigh to you" (James 4:8). This close relationship with our Creator ensures that we remain anchored in His love, capable of withstanding any trial.

In every challenge, remember that God's strength is our foundation. "The LORD is my light and my salvation; whom shall I fear? The LORD is the strength of my life; of whom shall I be afraid?" (Psalm 27:1). With God as our rock and fortress, we can face each day with confidence and courage, assured that this too shall pass.

As we continue this chapter in our lives, let us be encouraged by the knowledge that God is with us, providing strength, peace, and hope. "Be of good courage, and he shall strengthen your heart, all ye that hope in the

LORD" (Psalm 31:24). Trust in His promises and hold fast to your faith, knowing that a glorious future awaits us and His blessings are eternal.

May we remain steadfast, unshaken by the trials we face, and rooted deeply in the love and strength of our Almighty God. "Therefore, my beloved brethren, be ye steadfast, unmovable, always abounding in the work of the Lord, forasmuch as ye know that your labour is not in vain in the Lord" (1 Corinthians 15:58). Let us move forward with the confidence that every challenge we endure brings us closer to the fulfillment of God's glorious promises.

The wounds from the struggle, the piercing betrayal, and the harsh judgment we have endured and agonized over have led to significant growth in God. "But he knoweth the way that I take: when he hath tried me, I shall come forth as gold" (Job 23:10). Each trial and tribulation has refined us, shaping our character and deepening our faith.

These painful experiences, though difficult to bear, are not without purpose. "And we know that all things work together for good to them that love God, to them who are the called according to his purpose" (Romans 8:28). Through our endurance and perseverance, we have been prepared for greater blessings that we would not have received had we not endured these trials.

The growth we experience in our spiritual journey is often a direct result of our challenges. "My brethren, count it all joy when ye fall into divers temptations; knowing this, that the trying of your faith worketh patience. But let patience have her perfect work, that ye may be perfect and entire, wanting nothing" (James 1:2-4). The trials test our faith and build our resilience, making us stronger and more reliant on God's grace.

Reflecting on the pain and hardship, we see that each wound has brought us closer to God. "He healeth the broken in heart, and bindeth up their wounds" (Psalm 147:3). His healing power not only mends our hearts but also transforms our suffering into strength and wisdom.

Great blessings lie ahead, rewards born from our steadfast faith and perseverance. "Blessed is the man that endureth temptation: for when he is tried, he shall receive the crown of life, which the Lord hath promised to them that love him" (James 1:12). These blessings are a testament to God's faithfulness and the fulfillment of His promises.

In times of betrayal and judgment, we can take comfort in knowing God sees our pain and stands with us. "For we have not an high priest which cannot be touched with the feeling of our infirmities; but was in all points tempted like as we are, yet without sin" (Hebrews 4:15). Jesus understands our struggles and offers us His strength and compassion.

Hold fast to our faith, trusting God uses every experience to prepare us for His planned future. "For I know the thoughts that I think toward you, saith the LORD, thoughts of peace, and not of evil, to give you an expected end" (Jeremiah 29:11). His plans for us are always imbued with hope and promise.

As we continue this chapter in our lives, let us embrace the growth that comes from enduring hardships. "And let us not be weary in well doing: for in due season we shall reap, if we faint not" (Galatians 6:9). Our perseverance in the face of adversity brings us closer to God's blessings and the realization of His promises.

May we remain steadfast in our journey, confident that the struggles we endure today prepare us for tomorrow's triumphs. "But the God of all grace, who hath called us unto his eternal glory by Christ Jesus, after that ye have suffered a while, make you perfect, stablish, strengthen, settle you" (1 Peter 5:10). With God by our side, every trial is a step towards greater blessings and a deeper understanding of His love.

It takes a strong soul with a real heart to smile in situations that should otherwise bring us to tears. This strength is a testament to the resilience God so gracefully cultivates within us. "The LORD is my strength and my shield; my heart trusted in him, and I am helped: therefore my heart greatly rejoiceth; and with my song will I praise him" (Psalm 28:7). No matter how long it takes, we must hold on to the promise that things will get better. Tough situations build warriors.

Life's toughest battles often shape the strongest warriors. "But they that wait upon the LORD shall renew their strength; they shall mount up with wings as eagles; they shall run, and not be weary; and they shall walk, and not faint" (Isaiah 40:31). Each challenge we face is an opportunity for growth, resilience, and the strengthening of our faith.

For those of us who sometimes don't understand why we go through certain trials, hold on. God has a plan, and He knows what He is doing. "For my thoughts are not your thoughts, neither are your ways my ways, saith the LORD. As the heavens are higher than the earth, so are my ways higher than your ways, and my thoughts more than your thoughts" (Isaiah 55:8-9). Though His Divine plan is beyond our understanding, it is always for our ultimate good.

In times of confusion and pain, may we find comfort in knowing God is in control. "Trust in the LORD with all thine heart; and lean not unto thine own understanding. In all thy ways acknowledge him, and he shall direct thy paths" (Proverbs 3:5-6). Our limited perspective cannot see the full picture, but God's infinite wisdom guides us through every situation.

No matter how dark the night may seem, dawn is coming. "Weeping may endure for a night, but joy cometh in the morning" (Psalm 30:5). This promise reminds us that our current struggles are temporary and better days are ahead. "For I reckon that the sufferings of this present time are not worthy to be compared with the glory which shall be revealed in us" (Romans 8:18).

God's plan includes every detail of our lives, even the most challenging ones. "For I know the thoughts that I think toward you, saith the LORD, thoughts of peace, and not of evil, to give you an expected end" (Jeremiah 29:11). This assurance allows us to trust in His timing and purpose, even when we cannot see the way forward.

As we face life's trials, let us be encouraged by the knowledge that every struggle is a step toward becoming the warriors God intends us to be. "And not only so, but we glory in tribulations also: knowing that tribulation worketh patience; and patience, experience; and experience, hope" (Romans 5:3-4). Each test of faith builds our character, strengthens our resolve, and deepens our hope.

Remember, this too shall pass. Hold on to the promise of God's unfailing love and His perfect plan. God provides grace through Christ Jesus to strengthen you for the journey ahead. Therefore, fear not and be courageous; God is forever on your side, preparing the way home.

Be blessed in the Lord always!

CHAPTER 3

CHANGE ON PURPOSE

DIRECT YOUR LIFE

""Trust in the Lord with all thine heart; and lean not unto thine own understanding. In all thy ways acknowledge him, and he shall direct thy paths." Proverbs 3:5-6, KJV

RECOGNIZING OUR ABUNDANT BLESSINGS is essential in a world where adversity often prevails. These blessings emerge from life's most challenging moments, transforming our lives despite our unworthiness. As it is written in James 1:17 (KJV), "Every good gift and every perfect gift is from above, and cometh down from the Father of lights, with whom is no variableness, neither shadow of turning." Acknowledging our blessings, especially during trials, helps us understand the depth of God's love and the intricacies of His plans for us.

There is a divine irony in how our greatest blessings emerge from our most trying circumstances. The enemy may design our downfall, but God repurposes these moments for our upliftment. As Genesis 50:20 (KJV) states, "But as for you, ye thought evil against me; but God meant it unto good, to bring to pass, as it is this day, to save much people alive." These transformative moments change the course of life entirely. From the depths of despair, we are catapulted into the light of a new beginning, crossing from death unto life, as described in John 5:24 (KJV), "Verily, verily, I say unto you, He that heareth my word, and believeth on him that sent me, hath everlasting life, and shall not come into condemnation; but is passed from death unto life."

Personal Transformation

"Thank God I am not who I used to be!" This declaration resonates with the joy of personal transformation, reminding us that we are called to make a significant impact. As Romans 12:2 (KJV) exhorts, "And be not conformed to this world: but be ye transformed by the renewing of your mind, that ye may prove what is that good, and acceptable, and perfect, will of God." We are summoned to be world changers, not world chasers. Philippians 3:14 (KJV) encourages us, "I press toward the mark for the prize of the high calling of God in Christ Jesus."

Before coming to Christ, many attempts to fill an intrinsic void deep inside with worldly pursuits. This emptiness remains insatiable by the things of the world. True contentment of the heart and soul can only be found in the One who created them. Ecclesiastes 1:8 (KJV) aptly states, "All things are full of labour; man cannot utter it: the eye is not satisfied with seeing, nor the ear filled with hearing." The journey to fill this void is often misguided, leading us to seek fulfillment in places that can never truly satisfy. In John 6:35 (KJV), Jesus declares, "I am the bread of life: he that cometh to me shall never hunger; and he that believeth on me shall never thirst."

Divine Calling and Purpose

Understanding that only our Creator can fill the void within us shifts our perspective and purpose. We realize that our lives have a divine calling far greater than the transient pleasures of the world. Colossians 3:2 (KJV) instructs, "Set your affection on things above, not on things on the earth." This realization empowers us to direct our lives with intention and purpose, aligning our actions with the greater good and divine will. As we embrace this purpose, we find that Philippians 4:13 (KJV) holds true, "I can do all things through Christ which strengtheneth me."

As we embark on this journey of purposeful change, let us embrace the abundant blessings bestowed upon us, even in our darkest hours. Let us transform from world chasers to world changers, filling the void within us with the divine purpose only our Creator can provide. In doing so, we will change our lives and inspire and impact the world around us. Romans 8:28 (KJV) reassures us, "And we know that all things work together for good to them that love God, to them who are the called according to his purpose." Let this be our guiding principle as we direct our lives with intention and purpose.

Grace and Mercy

The grace and mercy of God accompany us throughout every moment of our lives. As we journey through the ups and downs, we must recognize that we are never alone. God's presence is a constant, unwavering force, guiding and shielding us from harm. Psalm 23:6 (KJV) beautifully captures this promise: "Surely goodness and mercy shall follow me all the days of my life: and I will dwell in the house of the Lord forever." This scripture reassures us that no matter the circumstances, God's goodness and mercy are ever-present, surrounding us with His divine protection and love.

God's goodness, favor, and mercies are gifts we could never earn through our efforts. They are bestowed upon us purely by His grace. Ephesians 2:8-9 (KJV) reminds us, "For by grace are ye saved through faith; and that not of yourselves: it is the gift of God: not of works, lest any man should boast." Understanding this, we see that every blessing we receive is a testament to God's infinite generosity and love. We gain a deeper appreciation of these blessings on this side of grace. Despite our imperfections, God's grace remains steadfast, a constant source of hope and encouragement.

We must be grateful for the staying power of God, which has rescued us time and again, often from our mistakes. When we lacked the strength to make the right decisions or to let go of harmful distractions, God's mercy intervened. This divine intervention reflects His abiding commitment to our well-being. Psalm 91:11 (KJV) assures us, "For he shall give his angels charge over thee, to keep thee in all thy ways." This scripture highlights the extent of God's protection, placing His angels in charge of our safety, a pure act of mercy that is neither earned nor deserved.

Unchanging Love

God's love is unchanging and faithfully endures through life's challenges. Even when we falter in our faith, He remains steadfast. 2 Timothy 2:13 (KJV) states, "If we believe not, yet he abideth faithful: he cannot deny himself." This ever-dependable faithfulness is a testament to God's nature, ensuring that His love and support are always available to us. Throughout every trial and triumph, His faithfulness provides a steady anchor, reminding us that we are never abandoned or forgotten.

As we continue our journey of purposeful change, let us reflect on the abundant grace and mercy God bestows upon us daily. These blessings, though undeserved, testify to His boundless love and faithfulness. Let us be thankful for the subtle nudges of the Holy Spirit and the keeping power of God that has protected us time and again. Embrace the truth of Psalm 100:5 (KJV), "For the Lord is good; his mercy is everlasting; and his truth endureth to all generations." With this understanding, we can move forward confidently, knowing that God's grace and mercy will continue to sustain us and guide our every step.

Seeking Refuge in God

King David, a man after God's heart, understood the necessity of seeking God's mercy and refuge. In Psalm 57:1 (KJV), he cries out, "Be merciful unto me, O God, be merciful unto me: for my soul trusteth in thee: yea, in the shadow of thy wings will I make my refuge, until these calamities be overpast." David's heartfelt plea emphasizes trusting God's protection during life's fiercest storms. This image of taking refuge under God's wings symbolizes our ultimate safety and security in His divine presence.

Recently, the Holy Spirit imparted a message that urged us to reflect deeply: "Are you dwelling there?" This question challenges us to examine our spiritual posture and commitment to abide by God's will. Our protection and blessings often hinge on our obedience and alignment with God's purpose. Although God's grace is abundant and His mercy unbounded, stepping outside His will exposes us to unnecessary risks. It compels us to consider whether we live under His divine protection by staying close to His guidance.

God's protection is often conditional upon our obedience and faithfulness. Remaining within His will ensures that we stay under His divine covering. As stated in Deuteronomy 28:1-2 (KJV), "And it shall come to pass, if thou shalt hearken diligently unto the voice of the Lord thy God, to observe and to do all his commandments which I command thee this day, that the Lord thy God will set thee on high above all nations of the earth: and all these blessings shall come on thee, and overtake thee, if thou shalt hearken unto the voice of the Lord thy God." This passage underscores the importance of obedience in receiving God's protection and blessings.

Trusting God's Plan

Even when we stray from the path God has set for us, His undeserved grace and mercy often shield us from the full consequences of our actions. This unmerited favor should demonstrate God's boundless love and patience to us. As Lamentations 3:22-23 (KJV) declares, "It is of the Lord's mercies that we are not consumed because his compassions fail not. They are new every morning: great is thy faithfulness." These verses remind us that God's mercy is renewed daily, offering us continuous protection and the chance to realign with His will.

As we navigate through life, let us continuously seek refuge under the shadow of God's wings, placing our trust in His mercy and grace. Reflect on the Holy Spirit's challenge to dwell in God's presence and remain within His will, recognizing that our protection and blessings are intertwined with our obedience. Embrace the assurance of Isaiah 26:3 (KJV), "Thou wilt keep him in perfect peace, whose mind is stayed on thee: because he trusteth in thee." With this understanding, we can face life's storms confidently, knowing that God's unwavering protection and boundless mercy are ever-present, guiding and sustaining us each step.

Fleeting Pleasures of Sin

We must face the sobering reality that the pleasure derived from sin is temporary, lasting only for a brief season. Hebrews 11:25 (KJV) reminds us that choosing "to enjoy the pleasures of sin for a season" leads to fleeting satisfaction. This momentary enjoyment pales in comparison to the eternal consequences of sin. Revelation 20:15 (KJV) provides a stark warning: "And whosoever was not found written in the book of life was cast into the lake of fire." The eternal torment of hell stands in sharp contrast to the short-lived gratification of sin. Therefore, we must let go of sinful ways, seek God, and find refuge in His everlasting grace and mercy.

Turning away from the fleeting pleasures of sin and seeking refuge in God leads to true peace and security. Psalm 46:1 (KJV) declares, "God is our refuge and strength, a very present help in trouble." This verse reassures us that God is our protector, always ready to offer strength and help in times of need. By seeking refuge in Him, we align ourselves with His divine purpose and experience the peace that surpasses all understanding.

Divine Interventions and Detours

In our spiritual journey, it is essential to cultivate gratitude for the doors that God has closed. These closed doors, roadblocks, and detours are often acts of divine intervention meant for our protection and well-being. Proverbs 3:5-6 (KJV) advises, "Trust in the Lord with all thine heart; and lean not unto thine own understanding. In all thy ways acknowledge him, and he shall direct thy paths." This scripture encourages us to trust in God's wisdom, even when it leads to unexpected detours or the closing of opportunities we once desired. Each closed door is a testament to God's protective love and desire to guide us toward a path that leads to greater blessings.

Recognizing that God's detours are for our benefit helps us trust His divine plan. These detours steer us from paths that may lead to harm and guide us toward a future filled with hope and promise. Jeremiah 29:11 (KJV) reassures us, "For I know the thoughts that I think toward you, saith the Lord, thoughts of peace, and not of evil, to give you an expected end." Understanding this, we can embrace the closed doors and detours with gratitude, knowing they are part of God's greater plan for our lives. His divine guidance ensures we are always on the path to fulfillment and peace.

As we continue our journey of purposeful change, let us embrace the reality that the pleasures of sin are fleeting while the consequences are eternal. By letting go of sin and seeking refuge in God, we align ourselves with His divine protection and purpose. Cultivate gratitude for the doors God has closed, recognizing them as acts of His mercy and love. Embrace the detours and roadblocks, trusting they guide us toward a future filled with His blessings and peace. Psalm 84:11 (KJV) assures us, "For the Lord God is a sun and shield: the Lord will give grace and glory: no good thing will he withhold from them that walk uprightly." We can confidently move forward with this understanding, trusting in God's unwavering guidance and protection.

Letting Go of Attachments

Embarking on the journey of "letting go" of worldly attachments involves the inevitable loss of many aspects of our past. Through this process, we discover a deeper connection with God. As we release our grip on material and emotional dependencies, we begin to understand the true nature of our identity in Christ. Philippians 3:8 (KJV) captures this sentiment: "Yea doubtless, and I count all things but loss for the excellency of the knowledge of Christ Jesus my Lord: for whom I have suffered the loss of all things, and do count them but dung, that I may win

Christ." This scripture reminds us that the genuine gain lies in knowing Christ intimately, surpassing all worldly possessions and relationships.

The empty things we have pursued often include people detrimental to our well-being. These individuals, though seemingly important at the time, impaired our spiritual and personal growth. In His infinite wisdom, God rescues us by removing these toxic influences from our lives. Psalm 1:1 (KJV) advises, "Blessed is the man that walketh not in the counsel of the ungodly, nor standeth in the way of sinners, nor sitteth in the seat of the scornful." By heeding this wisdom, we are blessed with the removal of those who do not belong in our lives, clearing the path for genuine, enriching relationships.

Divine Timing and Relationships

God knows precisely who belongs in our lives and who does not. He strategically places people in our path for specific reasons and removes them for even greater purposes. Ecclesiastes 3:1 (KJV) reminds us, "To everything there is a season and a time to every purpose under the heaven." Trusting in God's timing and decisions about who enters and exits our lives is crucial for our spiritual growth and fulfillment. Holding onto people who are no longer meant to be in our lives only delays God's perfect plan. By releasing them, we make room for God's intended blessings and purposes.

Acknowledging that not everyone who enters our lives is a true friend is vital. Some people are adept at pretending, concealing their true intentions. Proverbs 27:6 (KJV) says, "Faithful are the wounds of a friend, but the kisses of an enemy are deceitful." Real situations can expose fake people, revealing their true nature. God, who sees and hears what we cannot, guides us to remove such pretenders from our lives. This divine intervention ensures that we are surrounded by authentic, supportive relationships that contribute to our growth and well-being.

Purposeful Replacements

God's wisdom in removing people from our lives comes with the promise of purposeful replacements. He introduces individuals who align with His divine plan for us. Isaiah 43:19 (KJV) assures us, "Behold, I will do a new thing; now it shall spring forth; shall ye not know it? I will even make a way in the wilderness and rivers in the desert." Trusting in God's process of removal and replacement aligns us with His will, leading to greater fulfillment and purpose. His new provisions are designed to nurture and elevate us, ensuring we walk the path He has prepared.

As we continue our journey of purposeful change, let us embrace the process of letting go of worldly attachments and toxic relationships. In doing so, we find our true identity in God. Recognize that God's divine wisdom guides who belongs in our lives and who does not. Trust in His timing and plan, knowing that real situations expose fake people, and God removes them for better relationships. Embrace the promise of Isaiah 43:19 (KJV) and confidently move forward, trusting God's perfect guidance and provision for our lives. With this trust, we can confidently navigate our journey, knowing that God's grace and mercy continually work for our ultimate good.

God's Transformative Power

God, in His infinite mercy and power, saves us and turns around situations that the enemy intended for our destruction. What was meant to harm us, God uses for our good. This truth is illustrated in Genesis 50:20 (KJV), where Joseph tells his brothers, "But as for you, ye thought evil against me; but God meant it unto good, to bring to pass, as it is this day, to save much people alive." No matter how dire the circumstances, God's transformative power is constantly at work, converting our trials into testimonies of His grace and sovereignty. This assurance provides us with hope and strength, knowing that every hardship has the potential to be a steppingstone toward greater blessings and divine purpose.

God promises to provide a way to escape every temptation and trial. 1 Corinthians 10:13 (KJV) reassures us, "There hath no temptation taken you but such as is common to man: but God is faithful, who will not suffer you to be tempted above that ye are able; but will with the temptation also make a way to escape, that ye may be able to bear it." This verse highlights God's faithfulness and His understanding of our human limitations. He ensures that we are never overwhelmed beyond our capacity. His provision of escape routes in our darkest moments underscores His unwavering commitment to our well-being, reminding us that we are never alone or without hope.

Romans 8:28 (KJV) beautifully encapsulates the assurance that "all things work together for good to them that love God, to them who are the called according to his purpose." This powerful promise confirms that no matter the circumstances, God orchestrates everything for our ultimate good and His divine purpose. Our love for God and our commitment to His calling ensure that every trial, every setback, and every challenge is woven into His grand design for our lives. This weaving brings forth blessings, character development, and spiritual growth, transforming our struggles into steppingstones toward fulfillment and divine alignment.

Supreme Authority

God reigns with supreme authority over the enemy. No force can thwart His plans or diminish His power. Psalm 47:8 (KJV) declares, "God reigneth over the heathen: God sitteth upon the throne of his holiness." This scripture reaffirms that God is sovereign and His dominion is unchallenged. The enemy may plot and scheme, but God's authority and power are absolute, ensuring His will prevails in every situation. This understanding provides us with unshakable confidence, knowing that the outcome is securely in God's hands and His plans for us are for good, not for harm, to give us a future and hope.

As we continue our journey of purposeful change, let us find strength and encouragement in the knowledge that God saves us and turns situations meant for our harm into opportunities for growth and testimony. Trust in His promise to provide a way of escape from every trial and temptation. Embrace the assurance that all things work together for good to those who love God and are called according to His purpose. Finally, rest in the confidence that God reigns supreme authority over the enemy, ensuring His divine plan for our lives will always prevail. With this understanding, we can move forward with courage and faith, knowing that God's grace and mercy are continually at work for our ultimate good. As Psalm 37:23-24 (KJV) affirms, "The Lord orders the steps of a good man: and he delighteth in his way. Though he falls, he shall not be utterly cast down: for the Lord upholds him with his hand." Trust in this divine guidance and protection as you navigate life's journey.

Acknowledging Captivity

Consider this deeply: before we can be saved from the empty pursuits we chase, which eventually become our prisons, we must first recognize that we are locked up and desire to break free. As John 8:32 (KJV) proclaims, "And ye shall know the truth, and the truth shall make you free." This realization is crucial; we must acknowledge our bondage and genuinely yearn for liberation from the darkness. The initial step towards salvation is understanding our captivity and expressing a sincere desire to escape. This heartfelt longing for freedom ignites God's transformative work in our lives.

We must deeply desire to emerge from our darkness to break free from the chains that bind us truly. The enemy deceives us by projecting dark things as beautiful, enticing us with illusions that ultimately lead to our downfall. As 2 Corinthians 11:14 (KJV) warns, "And no marvel; for Satan himself is transformed into an angel of light." These deceptive attractions lure us into a false sense of fulfillment but can never satisfy our soul's deep longing. We must see through these illusions and recognize them for what they are—traps designed to enslave our mind, body, and soul.

Recognizing Deceptions

The things we chase to fill our emptiness are illusions, deceptions crafted to trap us. They appear promising but fail to provide genuine satisfaction. John 10:10 (KJV) contrasts the enemy's intent with God's promise: "The thief cometh not, but for to steal, and to kill, and to destroy: I am come that they might have life, and that they might have it more abundantly." The enemy's lies create a perpetual cycle of dissatisfaction, keeping us imprisoned in our desires. We can only break free from this cycle and experience true fulfillment by seeking the truth in Christ.

There is no truth in the enemy; Satan is a liar and the father of lies. John 8:44 (KJV) declares, "Ye are of your father the devil, and the lusts of your father ye will do. He was a murderer from the beginning and abode not in the truth because there is no truth in him. When he speaketh a lie, he speaketh of his own: for he is a liar, and the father of it." Recognizing the enemy's nefarious nature helps us discern his deceptions and avoid traps. Satan's lies aim to keep us in bondage, but the truth of God's word sets us free.

Embracing Freedom

As we continue our journey of purposeful change, let us deeply consider our need for salvation from the empty things we chase. Please recognize that these pursuits become our prisons; we must genuinely desire to break free. Understand the enemy's deceptive tactics and seek true fulfillment in Christ, who promises abundant life. Embrace the truth of John 8:32 (KJV), "And ye shall know the truth, and the truth shall make you free," and reject the enemy's lies. By doing so, we can move forward with clarity and purpose, fully embracing the freedom and abundant life God so graciously offers.

Acknowledging our need for God's saving grace is paramount in this journey of spiritual growth. The enemy's deceptive allurements cannot fill the deep void within us. Instead, the truth and love of Christ bring genuine liberation and lasting joy. Let us remain vigilant and steadfast, discerning the enemy's lies and embracing the transformative power of God's truth.

Gratitude for Divine Provision

Let us wholeheartedly thank God for protecting us from what we thought we wanted and blessing us with what we didn't realize we needed. We often desire things that may not benefit us in our limited understanding. However, God's infinite wisdom ensures that we receive what truly nurtures our souls and aligns with His divine plan. Proverbs 16:9 (KJV) reminds us, "A man's heart deviseth his way: but the Lord directeth his steps." Trusting in God's guidance, we find His provision far exceeds our expectations, fulfilling our deepest needs.

Do not be afraid; stand firm, and God will deliver us. Exodus 14:13 (KJV) encourages us with these words: "And Moses said unto the people, Fear ye not, stand still, and see the salvation of the Lord, which he will shew to you today." In moments of fear and uncertainty, standing firm in our faith allows God to manifest His power and deliverance. Our steadfastness bespeaks our trust in His promises and ability to rescue us from adversity.

Healing and Salvation

Like Jeremiah, we, too, can cry out to God for healing and salvation. Jeremiah 17:14 (KJV) expresses this heartfelt plea: "Heal me, O Lord, and I shall be healed; save me, and I shall be saved: for thou art my praise." Turning to God in our need demonstrates our reliance on His divine intervention. He is our healer and savior, the one we praise for His boundless mercy and grace. Our faith in His healing power brings restoration and wholeness to our lives.

The Lord is our light and our salvation. Psalm 27:1 (KJV) proclaims, "The Lord is my light and my salvation; whom shall I fear? the Lord is the strength of my life; of whom shall I be afraid?" This powerful declaration reinforces that with God as our guiding light, we have nothing to fear. His presence illuminates our path, providing clarity and direction amidst life's uncertainties. In His light, we find strength, courage, and assurance.

The Word declares, "The Lord hath done great things for us; whereof we are glad" (Psalm 126:3 KJV). Reflecting on God's marvelous deeds fills our hearts with joy and gratitude. Acknowledging His great works in our lives encourages us to trust His goodness and faithfulness. Our joy is a testament to His unending love and the blessings He bestows upon us, even when we least expect them.

As we continue our journey of purposeful change, let us thank God for His divine protection and provision, recognizing that His blessings often surpass our understanding. Stand firm in faith, trusting God to deliver us from every trial. Like Jeremiah, cry out to God for healing and salvation, knowing He is our source of praise. Embrace the Lord as our light and salvation, finding strength and courage in His presence. Rejoice in the great things He has done for us, filling our hearts with joy and gratitude. With this assurance, we can confidently move forward, knowing that God's grace and mercy guide and sustain us every step of the way.

Never underestimate the power of our testimony of God's grace and deliverance. Our personal stories of how God has transformed our lives are potent weapons against the enemy. Revelation 12:11 (KJV) declares, "And they overcame him by the blood of the Lamb, and by the word of their testimony; and they loved not their lives unto the death." This scripture underscores the dual power of Christ's sacrifice and our spoken witness in defeating the forces of darkness.

The Power of Testimony

We triumph over the enemy by the blood of the Lamb and by the word of our testimony. The blood of Jesus, shed on the cross, is the foundation of our victory. It signifies the ultimate sacrifice that redeems us from sin and grants us eternal life. Coupled with this, our testimonies serve as living proof of God's ongoing work in our lives. When we share how God's grace has delivered us from trials and temptations, we reinforce our faith and inspire others.

Our testimonies are not mere stories but declarations of God's power, love, and faithfulness. Each testimony is a beacon of hope, illuminating the path for struggling others. By recounting our experiences, we remind ourselves and others that God is always present, working, and victorious. Acts 1:8 (KJV) says, "But ye shall receive power, after that the Holy Ghost is come upon you: and ye shall be witnesses unto me." This verse highlights the empowerment of sharing our faith and its transformative effect on the world around us.

When we share our testimonies, we encourage others facing similar battles. Our stories of deliverance and grace provide tangible evidence of God's love and power. They serve as reminders that no situation is too difficult for God to handle. 2 Corinthians 1:4 (KJV) tells us, "Who comforteth us in all our tribulation, that we may be able to comfort them which are in any trouble, by the comfort wherewith we ourselves are comforted of God." By sharing how God has comforted and delivered us, we extend that same comfort to others.

Strength in Witnessing

Our testimonies not only inspire others but also weaken the enemy's hold. When we boldly proclaim what God has done in our lives, we strip the enemy of his power to deceive and discourage. Ephesians 6:12 (KJV) reminds us,

"For we wrestle not against flesh and blood, but against principalities, against powers, against the rulers of the darkness of this world, against spiritual wickedness in high places." In this spiritual battle, our testimonies are powerful tools that dismantle the enemy's strongholds and affirm our victory in Christ.

As we continue our journey of purposeful change, let us never underestimate the power of our testimony. By sharing how God's grace and deliverance have transformed our lives, we wield a powerful weapon against the enemy. Remember Revelation 12:11 (KJV), "And they overcame him by the blood of the Lamb, and by the word of their testimony." Embrace the power of your story, knowing that it can inspire, encourage, and lead others to victory. With this confidence, we can boldly declare God's goodness and stand firm in our faith, knowing that we triumph through Christ's sacrifice and spoken witness.

We are called to give testimony and be witnesses of Jesus Christ. Our stories of His grace and mercy can lead others to the truth, showing them salvation. Matthew 5:16 (KJV) encourages us, "Let your light so shine before men, that they may see your good works, and glorify your Father which is in heaven." By sharing our experiences, we illuminate the path for lost people, guiding them toward the light of Christ.

In our testimonies, we have the opportunity to lead someone to Christ. By showing them the way, we fulfill the Great Commission, as stated in Matthew 28:19 (KJV): "Go ye therefore, and teach all nations, baptizing them in the name of the Father, and of the Son, and of the Holy Ghost." Through our witness, we become vessels of God's love and instruments of His salvation, bringing hope and life to those in darkness. Our testimonies can spark faith in others, encouraging them to seek the transformative power of Jesus Christ.

"Thank you, sweet Jesus, for blessing us much more than we ever deserve!" This heartfelt gratitude acknowledges the countless blessings God has poured into our lives. Ephesians 3:20 (KJV) reminds us, "Now unto him that can do exceeding abundantly above all that we ask or think, according to the power that worketh in us." God's generosity surpasses our understanding, and His blessings often come in ways we could never have imagined. Recognizing His abundant grace fills our hearts with thankfulness and deepens our faith.

Transformative Power of Christ

"Thank God we are not who we used to be!" This powerful statement celebrates the transformative work of Christ in our lives. 2 Corinthians 5:17 (KJV) declares, "Therefore if any man be in Christ, he is a new creature: old things are passed away; behold, all things are become new." Our past no longer defines us; instead, we are renewed and redeemed through the love and sacrifice of Jesus. This transformation is only possible by God's grace and is a source of inspiration for others seeking change. By sharing our journey, we offer hope to those yearning for a fresh start and a new identity in Christ.

As we continue our journey of purposeful change, let us embrace the call to give testimony and be witnesses of Jesus Christ. By sharing our stories, we can lead others to the truth and show them salvation. Express heartfelt gratitude for our blessings, acknowledging that we are blessed beyond measure. Celebrate the transformative power of Christ, recognizing that we are no longer who we used to be. With this assurance, we can move forward confidently, knowing that our testimonies can inspire, encourage, and lead others to God's abundant life. Let us shine our light brightly, guiding others to the love and grace of our Savior.

Be blessed in the Lord always!

CHAPTER 4

RUN TO GOD
WIN THE RACE

"Know ye not that they which run in a race run all, but one receiveth the prize? So run, that ye may obtain."(1 Corinthians 9:24)

L IFE OFTEN ENTANGLES US in its mess, leading to times of trouble, pain, and hurt. In these moments, instead of turning to the world for answers, which ultimately leaves us empty and confused, we must run to God—our only true source of wisdom and peace.

When life's troubles arise, our first instinct is often to seek solutions in the world. Proverbs 14:12 (KJV) warns, "There is a way which seemeth right unto a man, but the end thereof are the ways of death." The world, however, only offers temporary fixes and fleeting comforts that do not address the root of our pain. God alone can provide the lasting peace and solutions we desperately need. Turning to Him in times of distress ensures that we seek wisdom from the One who truly understands our struggles and has the power to heal.

Sometimes, in our confusion and pain, we run away from God, mistakenly believing that distance will ease our discomfort or pain. However, Psalm 139:7-10 (KJV) reassures us, "Whither shall I go from thy spirit? or whither shall I flee from thy presence? If I ascend up into heaven, thou art there: if I make my bed in hell, behold, thou art there. If I take the wings of the morning, and dwell in the uttermost parts of the sea; Even there shall thy hand lead me, and thy right hand shall hold me." This passage reminds us that no matter how far we run, we can never escape God's presence. His love and protection are ever-present, ready to lead and hold us through our darkest times.

Instead of fleeing from God, we must learn to run *toward* Him. Hebrews 12:1-2 (KJV) encourages us to "lay aside every weight, and the sin which doth so easily beset us, and let us run with patience the race that is set before us, looking unto Jesus the author and finisher of our faith; who for the joy that was set before him endured the cross, despising the shame, and is set down at the right hand of the throne of God." Turning to God gives us the strength and wisdom to endure our struggles. Fixing our eyes on Jesus empowers us to overcome any obstacle, as His example of perseverance and faithfulness is our perfect model.

God promises to be our refuge in times of trouble. Psalm 46:1 (KJV) declares, "God is our refuge and strength, a very present help in trouble." By running to Him, we find a safe place to rest, heal, and receive guidance. In God's presence, the storms of life lose their power over us, and we find peace that surpasses all understanding (Philippians 4:7 KJV). His protection is unwavering, and His constant support assures us we are never alone.

As we embark on this journey of purposeful change, let us always run to God and not to the fleeting promises of the world. Embrace the truth that we can never outrun the hand of God, and His reach is always there to guide, protect, and comfort us. With patience and faith, let us run the race set before us, looking to Jesus, the author and finisher of our faith. Doing so gives us the strength and wisdom to overcome life's challenges and find the peace only God can provide.

Many pursue the glittering distractions of the world, only to find themselves slamming headfirst into difficulty and turmoil. Matthew 6:19-20 (KJV) warns, "Lay not up for yourselves treasures upon earth, where moth and rust doth corrupt, and where thieves break through and steal: But lay up for yourselves treasures in heaven, where neither moth nor rust doth corrupt, and where thieves do not break through nor steal." Instead of chasing after temporary treasures, we should wholeheartedly pursue the kingdom of God and His righteousness.

Our primary focus should be directing our steps toward the Kingdom of God with all our hearts. Matthew 6:33 (KJV) instructs, "But seek ye first the kingdom of God, and his righteousness; and all these things shall be added unto you." We discover a deeper sense of purpose and fulfillment when we prioritize our spiritual pursuits and align our lives with God's will. God promises to care for our needs when we place Him first, leading to a life of peace, joy, and eternal rewards far surpassing any worldly gain.

Those around us often influence us. Proverbs 13:20 (KJV) advises, "He that walketh with wise men shall be wise: but a companion of fools shall be destroyed." Our associations shape our thoughts and actions, so we must choose our companions wisely. Surrounding ourselves with godly influences helps us stay focused on our spiritual journey and strengthens our resolve to live according to God's will.

Philippians 4:8 (KJV) urges us to guard our minds and hearts against negative influences: "Finally, brethren, whatsoever things are true, whatsoever things are honest, whatsoever things are just, whatsoever things are pure, whatsoever things are lovely, whatsoever things are of good report; if there be any virtue, and if there be any praise, think on these things." By filling our thoughts with things that honor God, we remain steadfast in our faith and fortify ourselves against worldly distractions.

As we continue our journey of purposeful change, let us be mindful of the paths we choose and the influences we allow into our lives. Instead of chasing after fleeting treasures, let us run with all our hearts toward the Kingdom of God and His righteousness. Recognize the significant impact of those around us, and very deliberately choose to surround ourselves with people who inspire and uplift our faith. Guard our minds and hearts, focusing on what is true, honest, just, pure, lovely, and praiseworthy. By doing so, we align ourselves with God's will and ensure that our lives reflect His glory and grace.

Running into God's arms assures us of His presence and power in our lives. Isaiah 40:31 (KJV) promises, "But they that wait upon the Lord shall renew their strength; they shall mount up with wings as eagles; they shall run, and not be weary; and they shall walk, and not faint." This Divine promise encourages us, reminding us that God's presence invigorates us, allowing us to persevere through even the most grueling times.

Psalm 16:11 (KJV) declares, "Thou wilt shew me the path of life: in thy presence is fulness of joy; at thy right hand there are pleasures for evermore." We find His fullness of joy and eternal pleasures in God's presence that the world cannot offer. His power transforms our weaknesses into strengths and our fears into faith, providing a solid foundation of confidence and peace.

God tells us to run, not grow weary, to walk, and not faint. Philippians 4:13 (KJV) reinforces this truth: "I can do all things through Christ which strengtheneth me." In Christ, we find the resilience and energy to keep moving forward, even when the journey becomes tough. His strength is perfect in our weakness, allowing us to endure and overcome.

Deuteronomy 31:6 (KJV) assures us, "Be strong and of a good courage, fear not, nor be afraid of them: for the Lord thy God, he it is that doth go with thee; he will not fail thee, nor forsake thee." This powerful assurance reminds us that we are never alone in our struggles. God's unfailing presence and steadfast support allow us to press on, no matter our obstacles. Nothing is ever too big for God!

As we continue our journey of purposeful change, let us throw ourselves into God's arms, finding assurance in His presence and power. Embrace the Divine promise that we can run and not grow weary, walk, and not faint, as His strength and encouragement sustain us through life's grueling times. Trust in God's unwavering support, knowing that His presence brings fullness of joy and His power enables us to overcome.

God's Word declares that we must lay aside every weight that so easily besets us. Hebrews 12:1 (KJV) urges, "Wherefore seeing we also are compassed about with so great a cloud of witnesses, let us lay aside every weight, and the sin which doth so easily beset us, and let us run with patience the race that is set before us." These weights and sins hinder our progress and slow our spiritual journey. By casting them off, we free ourselves to run the race God has set before us with renewed vigor and determination.

Running the race before us with endurance requires patience and perseverance. Life's journey is not a sprint but a marathon, demanding sustained effort and unwavering faith. Galatians 6:9 (KJV) encourages us, "And let us not be weary in well doing: for in due season we shall reap, if we faint not." This promise reassures us that our perseverance will be rewarded in God's perfect timing. Every step taken in faith brings us closer to fulfilling His promises.

Patience is essential in our walk with God. James 1:4 (KJV) tells us, "But let patience have her perfect work, that ye may be perfect and entire, wanting nothing." Patience enables us to endure trials without losing hope. It teaches us to trust in God's timing and plan for our lives. We develop a mature, steadfast faith that stands firm in all circumstances by embracing patience.

We must not become beaten down or discouraged, for in due season, we will reap if we do not give up. Galatians 6:9 (KJV) is a powerful reminder that persistence in well-doing is key to reaping the harvest of blessings God has prepared for us. Our efforts and endurance are not in vain. Every act of faith, every moment of perseverance, brings us closer to the manifestation of God's promises.

Run to God with everything you've got! Proverbs 3:5-6 (KJV) advises, "Trust in the Lord with all thine heart; and lean not unto thine own understanding. In all thy ways acknowledge him, and he shall direct thy paths." When we wholeheartedly seek God, we find the strength, guidance, and support needed to navigate life's challenges. Running to God with all our hearts means fully surrendering to His will and trusting Him with every aspect of our lives. No exceptions.

As we continue our journey of purposeful change, let us heed the call to lay aside every weight and sin that hinders us. Run the race before us with endurance, embracing patience and perseverance. Do not become discouraged, for in due season, we will reap if we do not give up. Let us run to God with everything we've got, trusting Him with all our hearts. By doing so, we align ourselves with His Divine purpose and experience the transformative power of His grace and mercy.

Our strength comes from our prayer life and spending significant time praising and worshipping our Lord wholeheartedly. Studying God's Word daily is also essential. By feeding and nourishing our souls with His Word, we set our souls on fire with His Spirit, enabling us to live a vibrant and victorious Christian life.

Prayer is the lifeline that connects us directly to God. Philippians 4:6-7 (KJV) instructs us, "Be careful for nothing; but in every thing by prayer and supplication with thanksgiving let your requests be made known unto God. And the peace of God, which passeth all understanding, shall keep your hearts and minds through Christ Jesus." Through prayer, we bring our needs, concerns, and gratitude before the Lord, receiving His peace and strength in return.

Praising and worshipping God wholeheartedly is another vital aspect of our spiritual strength. Psalm 100:2 (KJV) exhorts, "Serve the Lord with gladness: come before his presence with singing." When we immerse ourselves in genuine worship, we experience God's presence. Worship shifts our focus from our weaknesses and problems to the greatness of our God, filling us with joy and strength.

Studying God's Word daily is crucial for our spiritual nourishment and growth. 2 Timothy 2:15 (KJV) advises, "Study to shew thyself approved unto God, a workman that needeth not to be ashamed, rightly dividing the word of truth." The Bible is our guidebook for life, providing wisdom, direction, and encouragement. Delving into Scripture regularly deepens our understanding of God's will and fortifies our faith.

Feeding and nourishing our souls with God's Word and His Spirit ignites a passion within us. Jeremiah 20:9 (KJV) captures this enthusiasm: "But his word was in mine heart as a burning fire shut up in my bones, and I was weary with forbearing, and I could not stay." Immersing ourselves in Scripture and the Holy Spirit fills us with Divine energy and purpose.

Setting our soul on fire with God's Word and Spirit transforms our lives. Acts 1:8 (KJV) promises, "But ye shall receive power, after that the Holy Ghost is come upon you: and ye shall be witnesses unto me both in Jerusalem, and in all Judaea, and in Samaria, and unto the uttermost part of the earth." The Holy Spirit empowers us to live victoriously and to be effective witnesses for Christ.

As we continue our journey of purposeful change, let us draw strength from our prayer life, praise and worship God wholeheartedly, and study His Word daily. By feeding and nourishing our souls with His Word and Spirit, we set our souls on fire, igniting a passion for God that transforms our lives and empowers us to live victoriously. Embrace these practices with dedication and faith, knowing that God's presence and power sustain us every step of the way.

We live according to God's purpose and promises when we walk by faith and not by sight. 2 Corinthians 5:7 (KJV) reminds us, "For we walk by faith, not by sight." Trusting in God's promises aligns us with His Divine plan even when we cannot see the path ahead.

Walking by faith means consistently trusting God's guidance and provision, even when the way forward is unclear. Hebrews 11:1 (KJV) defines faith as "the substance of things hoped for, the evidence of things not seen." This faith anchors us in God's promises, assuring us that He is with us and will never forsake us.

Being in alignment with God ensures that our hearts are right with Him. Psalm 37:23 (KJV) declares, "The steps of a good man are ordered by the Lord: and he delighteth in his way." This alignment brings peace and purpose as His wisdom and love guide us.

We must focus on God and the things above. Isaiah 26:3 (KJV) promises, "Thou wilt keep him in perfect peace, whose mind is stayed on thee: because he trusteth in thee." Focusing our thoughts on God and His promises shields us from the world's useless and harmful distractions and anxieties.

Run hard to God with all our hearts. Proverbs 3:5-6 (KJV) instructs, "Trust in the Lord with all thine heart; and lean not unto thine own understanding. In all thy ways acknowledge him, and he shall direct thy paths." This wholehearted pursuit of God requires dedication and trust, knowing He will guide and sustain us.

As we continue our journey of purposeful change, let us live according to God's purpose and promises by walking by faith and not by sight. Align our hearts with God, ensuring that our spirit, soul, and body work together in peace and harmony. Keep our minds focused on God and the things above, trusting Him to bring about perfect peace. Run hard to God with all our hearts, embracing His guidance and strength.

As the Apostle Paul encourages us, we must not run aimlessly. In 1 Corinthians 9:26 (KJV), Paul states, "I therefore so run, not as uncertainly; so fight I, not as one that beateth the air." We are called to run with purpose, dedication, devotion, and discipline.

Running with dedication and devotion means committing ourselves wholly to God's calling. Hebrews 12:1 (KJV) encourages us, "Wherefore seeing we also are compassed about with so great a cloud of witnesses, let us lay aside every weight, and the sin which doth so easily beset us, and let us run with patience the race that is set before us."

Endurance is essential for our spiritual journey. Matthew 24:13 (KJV) reminds us, "But he that shall endure unto the end, the same shall be saved." Endurance is cultivated by being rooted and grounded in God and His Word. Ephesians 3:17 (KJV) says, "That Christ may dwell in your hearts by faith; that ye, being rooted and grounded in love."

Standing firm in God and His Word is indispensable for running the race set before us. Psalm 119:105 (KJV) declares, "Thy word is a lamp unto my feet, and a light unto my path." God's Word provides the guidance and wisdom to navigate our spiritual journey.

We are called to run the highway of holiness. Isaiah 35:8 (KJV) describes this path, "And an highway shall be there, and a way, and it shall be called The way of holiness; the unclean shall not pass over it; but it shall be for those: the wayfaring men, though fools, shall not err therein." This path requires us to pursue holiness in all aspects of our lives. Hebrews 12:14 (KJV) reminds us, "Follow peace with all men, and holiness, without which no man shall see the Lord."

As we continue our journey of purposeful change, let us heed the Apostle Paul's exhortation to run with purpose, dedication, devotion, and discipline. We must endure, rooted and grounded in God and His Word. Run the race set before us, traversing the highway of holiness. Embrace the truth that without holiness, no man shall see the Lord.

We must put one foot in front of the other, acknowledging God in all things and believing every word that proceeds out of the mouth of God. Proverbs 3:5-6 (KJV) instructs us, "Trust in the Lord with all thine heart; and lean not unto thine own understanding. In all thy ways acknowledge him, and he shall direct thy paths."

Believing every word that proceeds from the mouth of God is essential for our spiritual growth and stability. Matthew 4:4 (KJV) reminds us, "But he answered and said, It is written, Man shall not live by bread alone, but by every word that proceedeth out of the mouth of God."

Paul taught the importance of modeling our lives after the Lord Jesus Christ. In 1 Corinthians 11:1 (KJV), Paul urges, "Be ye followers of me, even as I also am of Christ." Jesus is our perfect example, embodying the virtues of love, humility, obedience, and faith. By imitating Christ, we develop a character that reflects His grace and truth.

Walking in obedience to God's Word requires diligence and commitment. James 1:22 (KJV) exhorts us, "But be ye doers of the word, and not hearers only, deceiving your own selves." Obedience to God's commands demonstrates our faith and trust in Him. By walking in obedience, we experience the fullness of God's blessings and the joy of living in His purpose.

We must put one foot before the other, continually moving forward in faith. Philippians 3:13-14 (KJV) encourages, "Brethren, I count not myself to have apprehended: but this one thing I do, forgetting those things which are behind, and reaching forth unto those things which are before, I press toward the mark for the prize of the high calling of God in Christ Jesus."

As we continue our journey of purposeful change, let us acknowledge God in all things and believe every word from His mouth. Embrace the entirety of God's Word and model our lives after the Lord Jesus Christ. Follow His perfect example of love, humility, and obedience. Step forward in faith, trusting God to guide our paths and lead us to victory.

May we be fearless in this race, allowing it to set our souls on fire. Hebrews 12:1 (KJV) urges, "Wherefore seeing we also are compassed about with so great a cloud of witnesses, let us lay aside every weight, and the sin which doth so easily beset us, and let us run with patience the race that is set before us."

A soul on fire for God is a powerful weapon against the enemy. Ephesians 6:10-11 (KJV) commands, "Finally, my brethren, be strong in the Lord, and in the power of his might. Put on the whole armour of God, that ye may be able to stand against the wiles of the devil." This spiritual hunger equips us to stand firm and combat the enemy's relentless schemes.

We are called to relentlessly seek and pursue God. Jeremiah 29:13 (KJV) promises, "And ye shall seek me, and find me, when ye shall search for me with all your heart."

May we have fire in our souls and God's grace in our hearts. Romans 12:11 (KJV) exhorts, "Not slothful in business; fervent in spirit; serving the Lord."

A fire that we cannot contain and this world cannot snuff out is the mark of a life truly surrendered to God. Matthew 5:14-16 (KJV) declares, "Ye are the light of the world. A city that is set on a hill cannot be hid. Neither do men light a candle, and put it under a bushel, but on a candlestick; and it giveth light unto all that are in the house. Let your light so shine before men, that they may see your good works, and glorify your Father which is in heaven."

Let us run to God with all our hearts, fully devoted and wholly committed. Proverbs 3:5-6 (KJV) advises, "Trust in the Lord with all thine heart; and lean not unto thine own understanding. In all thy ways acknowledge him, and he shall direct thy paths."

As we continue our journey of purposeful change, may we be fearless in our race, allowing the fire of God to set our souls ablaze. Seek and pursue God fiercely, understanding that a soul on fire for Him is a formidable force against the enemy. Embrace the fire in our souls and His grace in our hearts, living with a passion that cannot be contained and a light that the world cannot extinguish. Run to God with all our hearts, trusting Him fully and acknowledging His guidance. By doing so, we align ourselves with His Divine purpose and experience the transformative power of His grace and mercy. With unwavering faith and dedication, we can confidently navigate life's challenges, knowing that God's presence and power sustain our every step.

Be blessed in the Lord always!

CHAPTER 5

STAY HUNGRY FOR GOD

CULTIVATE A PASSIONATE PURSUIT OF HIS PRESENCE

""Blessed are they which do hunger and thirst after righteousness: for they shall be filled."
(Matthew 5:6)

TO "STAY HUNGRY FOR GOD" means always seeking Him passionately and avoiding complacency that leads to spiritual stagnation. The Holy Spirit warns us that complacency is dangerous, pulling us away from a vibrant relationship with our

Creator. Losing our spiritual appetite sets us on a path to self-destruction.

The greater our hunger and thirst for God, the more His power and presence manifest in our lives. Matthew 5:6 (KJV) declares, "Blessed are they which do hunger and thirst after righteousness: for they shall be filled." This assurance confirms that those earnestly seeking God will be filled with His Spirit. A persistent pursuit of God unlocks deeper experiences of His grace and power.

There may be an obstruction if we do not feel God's presence. Isaiah 59:2 (KJV) warns, "But your iniquities have separated between you and your God, and your sins have hid his face from you, that he will not hear." We must carefully examine our hearts and lives to ensure we truly seek Him. Are we making space for God in our daily routines, thoughts, and actions? God dwells where He is sought, welcomed, and praised.

God promises to be found by those who diligently seek Him. Jeremiah 29:13 (KJV) says, "And ye shall seek me, and find me when ye shall search for me with all your heart." Our pursuit of God must be wholehearted and relentless. Our desire to grow in our relationship with God must surpass our comfort with the status quo. As a powerful reminder states, "Our desire to change must be greater than our desire to stay the same." This challenges us to constantly renew our commitment to pursuing God passionately.

When we stay hungry for God, we invite His transformative power into our lives. James 4:8 (KJV) assures us, "Draw nigh to God, and he will draw nigh to you." This promise encourages us to seek closeness with God, knowing He responds to our earnest pursuit. The more we seek Him, the more we experience His presence and power, transforming our lives.

As we embark on this journey, let us stay hungry for God. Be alert to new opportunities and driven by a passion to receive more of Him. Avoid complacency, recognizing that spiritual hunger leads to greater experiences of God's power and presence. Examine our hearts for obstructions and seek God with all our might. Embrace that our desire to change must be greater than our desire to stay the same. By staying hungry for God, we open ourselves to His grace and the transformative power of His presence. With unflinching dedication, let us pursue God relentlessly, confident that He will meet us and fill us with His Spirit.

Life unfolds differently for each of us. We must always submit to God's will if we face subtle shifts, great upheavals, surprises, or challenges. Proverbs 3:5-6 (KJV) instructs, "Trust in the Lord with all thine heart; and lean not unto thine own understanding. In all thy ways acknowledge him, and he shall direct thy paths." Our focus should remain on seeking God's righteousness rather than our desires.

We are called to hunger and thirst after God's righteousness. Matthew 5:6 (KJV) promises, "Blessed are they which do hunger and thirst after righteousness: for they shall be filled." When we earnestly seek God's ways, He satisfies our deepest spiritual needs. By aligning our desires with His, we open ourselves to His blessings and guidance.

We must cling to God's unchanging hand in times of change and uncertainty. Hebrews 13:8 (KJV) reminds us, "Jesus Christ the same yesterday, and today, and forever." God's nature and promises remain steadfast, providing a sure foundation upon which we can rely. His unwavering presence and faithfulness offer us security and comfort amidst life's unpredictability.

Believing and trusting in God's almighty power is crucial. Jeremiah 32:17 (KJV) proclaims, "Ah Lord God! behold, thou hast made the heaven and the earth by thy great power and stretched out arm, and there is nothing too hard for thee." Recognizing God's limitless power reassures us that He can handle any challenge we face. Faith in His power enables us to navigate life's difficulties with confidence and hope.

Submitting to God's will involves embracing His sovereignty over our lives. Romans 8:28 (KJV) states, "And we know that all things work together for good to them that love God, to them who are the called according to his purpose." Trusting in God's sovereign plan, we can rest assured that He orchestrates every event for our ultimate good and His glory. This trust allows us to face changes with a heart full of peace and assurance.

As we continue our journey of purposeful change, let us submit to God's will, hungering and thirsting after His righteousness. Hold tightly to His unchanging hand, believing and trusting in His almighty power. Embrace His sovereignty, knowing He works all things together for our good. By doing so, we align ourselves with His Divine purpose and experience the transformative power of His grace and mercy. With unwavering faith and dedication, we can confidently navigate life's challenges, knowing that God's presence and power sustain us every step of the way.

When we pursue God and truly hunger for Him, He prepares us for greater things. James 4:8 (KJV) encourages us, "Draw nigh to God, and he will draw nigh to you." Our sincere pursuit of God opens the door for His transformative work, equipping us with His greater plans.

We must commit to God daily and hunger for Him continually. Lamentations 3:22-23 (KJV) reminds us, "It is of the Lord's mercies that we are not consumed, because his compassions fail not. They are new every morning: great is thy faithfulness." Each new day is an opportunity to renew our commitment to God, to seek His presence, and to rely on His unfailing mercy and grace. Our daily commitment strengthens our relationship with Him and deepens our spiritual growth.

Every day, we have a choice: stay the same or seek something better. Deuteronomy 30:19 (KJV) presents this choice, "I call heaven and earth to record this day against you, that I have set before you life and death, blessing and cursing: therefore choose life, that both thou and thy seed may live." Choosing to pursue God and seek His righteousness is choosing life and blessing. It is a conscious decision to grow, improve, and align ourselves with God's will.

When we hunger for God and commit ourselves to Him, we embrace the miraculous transformation He offers. 2 Corinthians 5:17 (KJV) declares, "Therefore if any man be in Christ, he is a new creature: old things are passed away;

behold, all things are become new." This transformation is not just a one-time event but a continual process of renewal and growth. As we seek Him daily, He molds us into His image, preparing us for greater works and deeper experiences of His presence.

Our hunger for God should drive us to desire more of Him each day. Psalm 42:1 (KJV) beautifully expresses this longing: "As the hart panteth after the water brooks, so panteth my soul after thee, O God." This intense yearning for God motivates us to delve deeper into His Word, spend more time in prayer, and worship Him with all our hearts. This relentless pursuit draws us closer to Him and opens the way for His abundant blessings.

As we continue our journey of purposeful change, let us pursue God and truly hunger for Him, knowing that He prepares us for greater things. Commit to God daily, renewing our dedication and seeking His presence each morning. Recognize the power of our daily choices, choosing to grow and improve rather than staying the same. Embrace the transformation from being in Christ, desiring more of God daily. By doing so, we align ourselves with His Divine purpose and experience the transformative power of His grace and mercy. With unwavering faith and dedication, we can confidently navigate life's challenges, knowing that God's presence and power sustain us every step of the way.

At times, life blinds us when our direction abruptly changes. We must keep hope alive in our minds, hearts, and spirits in these moments. Romans 12:12 (KJV) encourages us to "Rejoice in hope; patient in tribulation; continuing instant in prayer." Maintaining hope anchors us in God's promises and sustains us through unexpected challenges.

In Jesus' name, we must rebuke the lies placed by the enemy. John 8:44 (KJV) reminds us, "Ye are of your father the devil, and the lusts of your father ye will do. He was a murderer from the beginning and abode not in the truth because there is no truth in him. When he speaketh a lie, he speaketh of his own: for he is a liar, and the father of it." Our mind is Satan's battleground; he will overtake it if we allow him. We must guard our thoughts and reject the enemy's deceptions, standing firm in the truth of God's Word.

Remember, Satan only has the power we give him. James 4:7 (KJV) instructs, "Submit yourselves therefore to God. Resist the devil, and he will flee from you." By submitting to God and resisting the devil, we fortify our minds against his attacks. Ephesians 6:11 (KJV) further exhorts us, "Put on the whole armour of God, that ye may be able to stand against the wiles of the devil." Clothed in God's armor, we can withstand the enemy's schemes and protect our minds from his pernicious influence.

Satan will try his best to derail us as his evil rages in the winds surrounding us. 1 Peter 5:8 (KJV) warns, "Be sober, be vigilant; because your adversary the devil, as a roaring lion, walketh about, seeking whom he may devour." We must remain vigilant, aware of the enemy's tactics, and steadfast in our faith. Our unflagging trust in God strengthens our resilience in spiritual warfare.

The Lord Almighty knows all and sees all. Psalm 121:3-4 (KJV) assures us, "He will not suffer thy foot to be moved: he that keepeth thee will not slumber. Behold, he that keepeth Israel shall neither slumber nor sleep." God's watchful eye is always upon us, providing protection and guidance. His omniscience and omnipotence give us confidence that He is in control no matter what life throws our way.

As we continue our journey of purposeful change, let us keep hope alive in our minds, hearts, and spirits, even when life's direction abruptly changes. Rebuke the lies of the enemy in Jesus' name, recognizing that our mind is a battleground he seeks to conquer. Remember that Satan only has the power we give him; resist his attempts to derail us by standing firm in God's truth. Trust in the Lord Almighty, who knows and sees all. By doing so, we align ourselves with His Divine purpose and experience the transformative power of His grace and mercy. With unwavering faith and dedication, we can confidently navigate life's challenges, knowing that God's presence and power sustain us every step of the way.

Sometimes, with great change, everything seems to be going against us. Opposition and resistance can feel overwhelming. Here's a good analogy: "When an airplane takes off, it goes against the wind, not with it." Even though it may seem like we are being punished, God is not punishing us—He is preparing us. Jeremiah 29:11 (KJV) reassures us, "For I know the thoughts that I think toward you, saith the Lord, thoughts of peace, and not of evil, to give you an expected end." We must trust His plan, not our pain.

Just as an airplane needs the wind's resistance to lift off, we often need opposition to strengthen and elevate us. James 1:2-4 (KJV) encourages, "My brethren, count it all joy when ye fall into divers temptations; knowing this, that the trying of your faith worketh patience. But let patience have her perfect work, that ye may be perfect and entire, wanting nothing." The trials we face are definite opportunities for growth and refinement, shaping us into the individuals God intends us to be.

We must trust God's purpose even when we don't understand what is happening. Proverbs 3:5-6 (KJV) instructs, "Trust in the Lord with all thine heart; and lean not unto thine own understanding. In all thy ways acknowledge him, and he shall direct thy paths." Our limited perspective cannot grasp the full extent of God's plans, but we can trust He is working all things for our good.

Hunger and thirst for His will in our lives. Matthew 5:6 (KJV) promises, "Blessed are they which do hunger and thirst after righteousness: for they shall be filled." This longing for God's will aligns our hearts with His, enabling us to receive His guidance and blessings. When we seek His will above our own, we open ourselves to the fullness of His grace and direction.

Jesus provides reassurance in times of uncertainty. John 13:7 (KJV) quotes Him saying, "Jesus answered and said unto him, What I do thou knowest not now; but thou shalt know hereafter." This promise reminds us that even if we do not understand His actions now, we will eventually see His purpose and wisdom. Trusting in Jesus' words brings great comfort and confidence as we navigate the unknown.

As we continue our journey of purposeful change, let us remember that opposition and resistance are part of God's preparation, not punishment. Embrace these challenges as opportunities for growth, trusting in God's greater plan. We hunger and thirst for His will, knowing He will fill us with His righteousness. Hold onto Jesus' reassurance that in time, we will surely understand what we do not understand now. By trusting in God's purpose and plan, we align ourselves with His Divine will and experience the transformative power of His grace and mercy. With unwavering faith and dedication, we can confidently navigate life's challenges, knowing that God's presence and power sustain us every step of the way.

God is always preparing and positioning us for Divine appointments. Ephesians 2:10 (KJV) declares, "For we are his workmanship, created in Christ Jesus unto good works, which God hath before ordained that we should walk in them." Every step of our journey is part of God's meticulous plan, guiding us to the right place at the right time for His purposes.

Prayer is the way we discern our next move. Philippians 4:6-7 (KJV) encourages us, "Be careful for nothing; but in every thing by prayer and supplication with thanksgiving let your requests be made known unto God. And the peace of God, which passeth all understanding, shall keep your hearts and minds through Christ Jesus." Through prayer, we seek God's guidance and peace, gaining clarity about His will for our lives. In prayer, we open our hearts to the promptings of the Holy Spirit, who leads us into God's perfect plan.

When God starts shifting the wind, we must be submissive and obedient in our new direction. Isaiah 30:21 (KJV) assures us, "And thine ears shall hear a word behind thee, saying, This is the way, walk ye in it, when ye turn to the right hand, and when ye turn to the left." Obedience to God's leading is crucial for stepping into the new places He has prepared for us. Even when the path is unfamiliar, our trust in His guidance will direct us safely.

As the Lord leads us to new places, we must allow our minds to be renewed. Romans 12:2 (KJV) instructs, "And be not conformed to this world: but be ye transformed by the renewing of your mind, that ye may prove what is that good, and acceptable, and perfect, will of God." Renewing our minds aligns our thoughts with God's, enabling us to understand and embrace His will. This transformation is essential for navigating new seasons with faith and confidence.

Our mind, heart, and spirit must continuously seek the Lord. Jeremiah 29:13 (KJV) promises, "And ye shall seek me, and find me when ye shall search for me with all your heart." A wholehearted pursuit of God positions us to receive His direction and blessings. This sincere seeking fosters a deeper relationship with Him, making us more attuned to His voice and more responsive to His leading.

We must want and desire what He wants for us. Psalm 37:4 (KJV) encourages, "Delight thyself also in the Lord; and he shall give thee the desires of thine heart." When our desires align with God's, He fulfills them in ways that exceed our expectations. This alignment comes from a heart fully devoted to seeking His will and a spirit willing to follow wherever He leads. As we continue our journey of purposeful change, let us recognize that God is always preparing and positioning us for Divine appointments. Through prayer, we discern our next move, and by being submissive and obedient, we follow His leading in new directions. Allow your mind to be renewed, aligning your thoughts with God's perfect will. Seek the Lord with all your mind, heart, and spirit, desiring what He wants for you. By doing so, you align yourself with His Divine purpose and experience the transformative power of His grace and mercy. With unwavering faith and dedication, you can confidently navigate life's changes, knowing that God's presence and power sustain you every step of the way.

Life is like the wind—sometimes "a sweet breeze" and at other times "a raging storm." We all need a strong foundation built on Jesus Christ our Lord. Amen! Matthew 7:24-25 (KJV) affirms this, "Therefore whosoever heareth these sayings of mine, and doeth them, I will liken him unto a wise man, which built his house upon a rock: and the rain descended, and the floods came, and the winds blew, and beat upon that house; and it fell not: for it was founded upon a rock."

Some anchor themselves down into a comfort zone, unwilling to move with the winds of change, finding themselves in a deep spiritual sleep—complacent and feeling dead inside. Revelation 3:1-2 (KJV) warns, "I know thy works, that thou hast a name that thou livest, and art dead. Be watchful, and strengthen the things that are ready to die: for I have not found thy works perfect before God." This spiritual stagnation prevents us from experiencing the fullness of God's plans for our lives.

God calls us out of those comfort zones, those dead sleep, and says, "Live!" Ezekiel 37:5 (KJV) prophesies, "Thus saith the Lord God unto these bones; Behold, I will cause breath to enter into you, and ye shall live." God's Word declares that we should consider ourselves dead to sin but alive to God in Christ Jesus. Romans 6:11 (KJV) states, "Likewise reckon ye also yourselves to be dead indeed unto sin, but alive unto God through Jesus Christ our Lord." This new life in Christ empowers us to break free from complacency and embrace His abundant life.

A strong foundation in Jesus Christ is essential for weathering life's storms. 1 Corinthians 3:11 (KJV) emphasizes, "For other foundation can no man lay than that is laid, which is Jesus Christ." By grounding our lives in Him, we ensure stability and resilience, no matter how fierce the winds of change may blow. This foundation keeps us anchored in truth and steadfast in faith.

We must be willing to move and adjust to the winds of change, trusting in God's direction. Isaiah 43:19 (KJV) encourages, "Behold, I will do a new thing; now it shall spring forth; shall ye not know it? I will even make a way in the wilderness and rivers in the desert." Embracing change requires faith in God's promises and a readiness to leave our comfort zones. Through this willingness to follow Him, we experience growth and transformation.

As we continue our journey of purposeful change, let us remember that life is like the wind—sometimes gentle, sometimes fierce. We need a strong foundation built on Jesus Christ to withstand the storms. Avoid the dangers of complacency, and respond to God's call to live. Build your life on the solid foundation of Christ, and be willing to embrace change with faith. By doing so, you align yourself with God's Divine purpose and experience the transformative power of His grace and mercy. With unwavering faith and dedication, you can confidently navigate life's changes, knowing that God's presence and power sustain you every step of the way.

God always prepares those who are willing to hunger and thirst after Him. Matthew 5:6 (KJV) promises, "Blessed are they that do hunger and thirst after righteousness: for they shall be filled." Our willingness to seek God with all our hearts opens the door for His Divine preparation and empowerment.

As willing vessels, we must crucify the flesh daily and die to sin. Galatians 5:24 (KJV) declares, "And they that are Christ's have crucified the flesh with the affections and lusts." This daily commitment to dying to our sinful nature and living in the Spirit is essential for true spiritual growth. Romans 8:13 (KJV) reinforces this, "For if ye live after the flesh, ye shall die: but if ye through the Spirit do mortify the deeds of the body, ye shall live." We allow the Holy Spirit to lead and transform us by crucifying our flesh.

Living in the Spirit is a powerful commitment for those who are sincere and true in their walk with God. Galatians 5:25 (KJV) instructs, "If we live in the Spirit, let us also walk in the Spirit." This means allowing the Holy Spirit to guide our thoughts, actions, and decisions daily. It is a conscious choice to follow God's leading and to align our lives with His will.

This commitment to living in the Spirit requires heartfelt dedication and perseverance. Luke 9:23 (KJV) reminds us, "And he said to them all, If any man will come after me, let him deny himself, and take up his cross daily, and follow me." True discipleship involves a daily decision to deny ourselves and follow Jesus wholeheartedly. It is a journey of continual surrender and obedience to God's will.

Embracing spiritual discipline is crucial for maintaining this commitment. 1 Corinthians 9:27 (KJV) says, "But I keep under my body, and bring it into subjection: lest that by any means when I have preached to others, I myself should be a castaway." Discipline in prayer, reading the Word, and seeking God's presence keeps our spiritual fervor alive and our focus on His purposes.

As we continue our journey of purposeful change, let us remember that God always prepares those who are willing. Hunger and thirst after Him and commit to crucifying the flesh daily. Live in the Spirit, making a powerful commitment to follow God sincerely and truly. Embrace spiritual discipline, allowing it to keep your focus on God's will. By doing so, you align yourself with His Divine purpose and experience the transformative power of His grace and mercy. With unwavering faith and dedication, you can confidently navigate life's changes, knowing that God's presence and power sustain you every step of the way.

The greatest enemy of our hunger for God is the temptation to "ride the fence" and nibble off the devil's table. Ouch, or Amen! God help us! This speaks truth to the heart of our spiritual struggle. Nibbling at what the devil offers dulls our appetite for heaven, weakening our resolve and dedication to God.

Fence riders and the lukewarm face serious warnings in Scripture. Revelation 3:15-16 (KJV) admonishes, "I know thy works, that thou art neither cold nor hot: I would thou wert cold or hot. So then, because thou art lukewarm and neither cold nor hot, I will spue thee out of my mouth." This vivid imagery underscores the gravity of spiritual complacency. God desires wholehearted commitment, not half-hearted devotion.

To maintain our spiritual enthusiasm, we must resist the temptation to compromise. James 4:4 (KJV) warns, "Ye adulterers and adulteresses, know ye not that the friendship of the world is enmity with God? whosoever therefore will be a friend of the world is the enemy of God." Our allegiance must be solely to God, consciously rejecting the world's distractions and temptations that lead us away from Him.

Cultivating a deep hunger for God requires intentional effort. Psalm 42:1 (KJV) expresses this longing, "As the heart panteth after the water brooks, so panteth my soul after thee, O God." We must actively seek God through prayer, worship, and studying His Word, allowing our desire for Him to grow and flourish.

Choosing commitment over compromise strengthens our faith and deepens our relationship with God. Matthew 6:24 (KJV) reminds us, "No man can serve two masters: for either he will hate the one, and love the other; or else he will hold to the one, and despise the other. Ye cannot serve God and mammon." Our lives should reflect resolute dedication to God, rejecting any form of spiritual compromise.

God calls us to wholehearted devotion. Deuteronomy 6:5 (KJV) commands, "And thou shalt love the Lord thy God with all thine heart, and with all thy soul, and with all thy might." This all-encompassing love for God demands our full attention and commitment, leaving no room for divided loyalties.

Resist the dangers of lukewarmness and spiritual complacency. Maintain your spiritual fervor by rejecting compromise and cultivating a deep hunger for God. Choose commitment over compromise, embracing the call to wholehearted devotion. By doing so, you align yourself with God's Divine purpose and experience the transformative power of His grace and mercy. With unwavering faith and dedication, you can confidently navigate life's challenges, knowing that God's presence and power sustain you every step.

The Holy Spirit always confirms His truth and guidance. As I reflected on this powerful journey, I came across a statement that resonates deeply with our spiritual walk: "There was a day when I died—died to self, my opinions, preferences, tastes, and will; died to the world, its approval or censure; died to the approval or blame even of my brethren or friends. Since then, I have studied only to show myself approved unto God." - George Müller

This powerful declaration reminds us of the importance of dying to self and the world. Galatians 2:20 (KJV) states, "I am crucified with Christ: nevertheless I live; yet not I, but Christ liveth in me: and the life which I now live in the flesh I live by the faith of the Son of God, who loved me, and gave himself for me." This transformation calls us to surrender our desires, opinions, and preferences, embracing God's will above all else.

George Müller's commitment to seeking only God's approval closely echoes the call in 2 Timothy 2:15 (KJV), "Study to shew thyself approved unto God, a workman that needeth not to be ashamed, rightly dividing the word of truth." Our focus should be on pleasing God rather than seeking the approval or acceptance of the world or even our close associates. This single-minded devotion leads to a deeper, more authentic relationship with the Lord.

To live a life fully surrendered to God requires a conscious decision to die to self, daily. Luke 9:23 (KJV) reminds us, "And he said to them all, If any man will come after me, let him deny himself, and take up his cross daily, and follow me." This daily act of self-denial and taking up our cross signifies our commitment to follow Christ wholeheartedly, no matter the cost.

Embracing this transformation leads to a life of freedom and purpose. Romans 12:1-2 (KJV) urges, "I beseech you therefore, brethren, by the mercies of God, that ye present your bodies a living sacrifice, holy, acceptable unto God, which is your reasonable service. And be not conformed to this world: but be ye transformed by the renewing of your mind, that ye may prove what is that good, and acceptable, and perfect, will of God." By renewing our minds and aligning our lives with God's will, we experience His perfect plan for us.

A life dedicated to God's approval becomes a powerful testimony. Philippians 3:7-8 (KJV) reflects this dedication: "But what things were gain to me, those I counted loss for Christ. Yea doubtless, and I count all things but loss for the excellency of the knowledge of Christ Jesus my Lord: for whom I have suffered the loss of all things, and do count them but dung, that I may win Christ." When we consider everything else as loss compared to knowing Christ, our lives become a testament to His grace and power.

As we continue our journey of purposeful change, let us embrace the call to die to self and the world, seeking only God's approval. Live a life of surrender, renewing your mind daily and aligning your actions with God's will. Allow this transformation to lead you into a deeper relationship with the Lord, becoming a powerful living testimony of His grace and mercy. With unwavering faith and dedication, navigate life's challenges confidently, knowing that God's presence and power will sustain you every step.

We must surround ourselves with those who intensify and encourage our hunger and appetite for God. Proverbs

27:17 (KJV) tells us, "Iron sharpeneth iron; so a man sharpeneth the countenance of his friend." A community fostering spiritual growth is essential for sustaining our passion for the Lord.

Are we anorexic in the spirit, starving for God? Matthew 4:4 (KJV) reminds us, "But he answered and said, It is written, Man shall not live by bread alone, but by every word that proceedeth out of the mouth of God." Just as physical nourishment is crucial for our bodies, spiritual nourishment is vital for our souls. We must feed on God's Word and seek His presence daily to avoid spiritual malnutrition.

We must die to our flesh, not our spirit. Galatians 5:24 (KJV) declares, "And they that are Christ's have crucified the flesh with the affections and lusts." By putting to death the deeds of the flesh, we allow our spirit to thrive and flourish. Crucifying the flesh is a daily commitment to living a life that truly honors God.

We are to live and declare the works of the Lord. Psalm 118:17 (KJV) proclaims, "I shall not die, but live, and declare the works of the Lord." Our lives should be a testament to God's goodness and faithfulness. By living in the Spirit and walking in His ways, we become living testimonies of His grace and power.

"I do hunger and thirst after righteousness! I do hunger and thirst after God's will!" Do you? Matthew 5:6 (KJV) promises, "Blessed are they which do hunger and thirst after righteousness: for they shall be filled." This longing for God's righteousness and will should be the driving force of our lives. When we earnestly seek Him, He satisfies our deepest spiritual desires.

As we continue our journey of purposeful change, let us surround ourselves with those who encourage and intensify our hunger for God. Avoid spiritual malnutrition by feeding on His Word and seeking His presence daily. Die to the flesh and allow your spirit to thrive. Live to declare the works of the Lord, becoming a living testament to His grace and power. Hunger and thirst after righteousness and God's will, knowing He will fill you. By doing so, you align yourself with His Divine purpose and experience the transformative power of His grace and mercy. With steadfast faith and dedication, you can confidently navigate life's challenges, knowing that God's presence and power sustain you every step.

A famous quote reminds us, "If we are not hungry for God, we are probably full of ourselves!" This truth calls us to self-examination and humility. James 4:6 (KJV) declares, "But he giveth more grace. Wherefore he saith, God resisteth the proud, but giveth grace unto the humble." We must empty ourselves of pride and self-righteousness to make room for a genuine hunger for God.

We must be aware of the wicked Jezebel spirit surrounding us—spirits of rebellion and self-righteousness. Revelation 2:20 (KJV) warns, "Notwithstanding I have a few things against thee, because thou sufferest that woman Jezebel, which calleth herself a prophetess, to teach and to seduce my servants to commit fornication, and to eat things sacrificed unto idols." This spirit fosters rebellion, pride, and a lack of accountability, leading us away from God's truth and humility.

Self-righteousness blinds us to our own shortcomings. Proverbs 30:12 (KJV) states, "There is a generation that are pure in their own eyes, and yet is not washed from their filthiness." We must be careful not to fall into the trap of believing we are without fault while failing to recognize our need for God's cleansing. True humility involves acknowledging our sins and seeking God's forgiveness.

Humility and accountability are essential for spiritual growth. 1 Peter 5:6 (KJV) instructs, "Humble yourselves therefore under the mighty hand of God, that he may exalt you in due time." By humbling ourselves and taking responsibility for our actions, we open the door for God's grace and transformation.

We must be careful, watchful, and sensitive to our discernment. Hebrews 5:14 (KJV) says, "But strong meat belongeth to them that are of full age, even those who by reason of use have their senses exercised to discern both good and evil." Developing spiritual discernment helps us navigate our challenges and overcome deceptions, keeping us aligned with God's will.

Push into God like never before. Have a genuine hunger for God. Psalm 63:1 (KJV) expresses this longing, "O God, thou art my God; early will I seek thee: my soul thirsteth for thee, my flesh longeth for thee in a dry and thirsty land, where no water is." This earnest seeking brings us closer to God, filling us with His presence and power.

Be blessed in the Lord always!

CHAPTER 6

HIS WILL NOT YOURS

SURRENDER TO GOD'S PLAN AND PURPOSE

"And he went a little farther, and fell on his face, and prayed, saying, O my Father, if it be possible, let this cup pass from me: nevertheless not as I will, but as thou wilt."
(Matthew 26:39)

A FAMOUS QUOTE REMINDS US, "If we are not hungry for God, we are probably full of ourselves!" This truth urges us toward self-examination and humility. James 4:6 (KJV) declares, "But he giveth more grace. Wherefore he saith, God resisteth the proud, but giveth grace unto the humble." To cultivate a genuine hunger for God, we must empty ourselves of pride and self-righteousness.

We must also be vigilant against the pernicious influence of the Jezebel spirit, which embodies rebellion and self-righteousness. Revelation 2:20 (KJV) warns, "Notwithstanding I have a few things against thee, because thou sufferest that woman Jezebel, which calleth herself a prophetess, to teach and to seduce my servants to commit fornication, and to eat things sacrificed unto idols." This spirit fosters rebellion, pride, and a lack of accountability, leading us away from God's truth and humility.

Self-righteousness blinds us to our shortcomings. Proverbs 30:12 (KJV) states, "There is a generation that is pure in their own eyes, and yet is not washed from their filthiness." We must avoid believing we are without fault while failing to recognize our need for God's cleansing. True humility involves acknowledging our sins and seeking God's forgiveness.

Humility and accountability are crucial for spiritual growth. 1 Peter 5:6 (KJV) instructs, "Humble yourselves under the mighty hand of God, that he may exalt you in due time." By humbling ourselves and taking responsibility for our actions, we open the door for God's grace and transformation.

We must be discerning and vigilant. Hebrews 5:14 (KJV) says, "But strong meat belongeth to them that are of full age, even those who by reason of use have their senses exercised to discern both good and evil." Developing spiritual discernment helps us navigate our challenges and deceptions, keeping us aligned with God's will.

Earnestly seek God with a genuine hunger. Psalm 63:1 (KJV) expresses this longing, "O God, thou art my God; early will I seek thee: my soul thirsteth for thee, my flesh longeth for thee in a dry and thirsty land, where no water is." This earnest seeking brings us closer to God, filling us with His presence and power.

God does not ask us to try harder; He wants us to trust Him deeper. Proverbs 3:5-6 (KJV) teaches, "Trust in the Lord with all thine heart; and lean not unto thine own understanding. In all thy ways acknowledge him, and he shall direct thy paths." Trusting in God means relying on His wisdom and timing rather than our efforts.

When we trust God, we do not have to force anything. It happens naturally as He sees fit. Psalm 37:5 (KJV) reassures us, "Commit thy way unto the Lord; trust also in him; and he shall bring it to pass." This Divine assurance reminds us that God's plans unfold perfectly in His perfect timing when we place our faith in Him. Our striving and self-effort cannot accomplish what God's grace can.

We must have complete confidence in the Divinely appointed plan for our lives. Jeremiah 29:11 (KJV) promises, "For I know the thoughts that I think toward you, saith the Lord, thoughts of peace, and not of evil, to give you an expected end." God's intentions for us are always for our good, designed to bring us into a future filled with hope and fulfillment.

Surrendering to God's plan requires deep trust and relinquishing control to Him alone. Isaiah 26:3-4 (KJV) states, "Thou wilt keep him in perfect peace, whose mind is stayed on thee: because he trusteth in thee. Trust ye in the Lord for ever: for in the Lord Jehovah is everlasting strength." This perfect peace comes from a steadfast mind fixated on God's faithfulness and strength.

Living by faith rather than sight transforms our approach to life's challenges. Hebrews 11:1 (KJV) defines faith as "the substance of things hoped for, the evidence of things not seen." Faith is not about seeing the whole path ahead but trusting that God has laid it out perfectly. When we walk by faith, our journey becomes one of confidence and peace.

Embracing God's timing is key to trusting Him deeper. Ecclesiastes 3:1 (KJV) tells us, "To everything there is a season, and a time to every purpose under the heaven." Recognizing that God orchestrates life's seasons helps us rest in His timing and trust His process.

As we continue our journey of purposeful change, let us shift from trying harder to trusting God deeper. Place all of your confidence in His Divinely appointed plan for your life. Trust in His timing and His ways, knowing that His plans for you are good. Surrender control, live by faith, and embrace the peace from trusting God's everlasting strength. By doing so, you align yourself with His Divine purpose and experience the transformative power of His grace and mercy. With unwavering faith and dedication, you can confidently navigate life's challenges, knowing that God's presence and power sustain you every step.

The level of power we operate in depends on how much our self-will diminishes. John 3:30 (KJV) reminds us, "He must increase, but I must decrease." Submitting our will to God's will marks the beginning of a journey filled with victory after victory. When we submit our heart, mind, and spirit to God's will, He performs great and mighty things in and through us.

Surrendering to God's will is the gateway to experiencing His abundant blessings. Luke 22:42 (KJV) captures the essence of true surrender: "Saying, Father, if thou be willing, remove this cup from me: nevertheless not my will, but thine, be done." We open ourselves to His transformative power when we align our desires with God's purposes.

God promises to fill us with joy that is unspeakable and full of glory. 1 Peter 1:8 (KJV) declares, "Whom having not seen, ye love; in whom, though now ye see him not, yet believing, ye rejoice with joy unspeakable and full of glory." This Divine joy transcends our current circumstances and fills our hearts with heavenly delight.

The Lord gives us peace that surpasses all understanding. Philippians 4:7 (KJV) assures us, "And the peace of God, which passeth all understanding, shall keep your hearts and minds through Christ Jesus." This peace guards our hearts and minds, providing serene assurance that God is in control, regardless of the chaos around us.

When we submit fully to God and declare, "Nevertheless not my will, but thine be done," He transforms every area of our lives. Romans 12:1-2 (KJV) urges, "I beseech you therefore, brethren, by the mercies of God, that ye present your bodies a living sacrifice, holy, acceptable unto God, which is your reasonable service. And be not conformed to this world: but be ye transformed by the renewing of your mind, that ye may prove what is that good, and acceptable, and perfect, will of God." This transformation aligns our lives with God's perfect will, bringing about lasting change.

As we continue our journey of purposeful change, let us embrace the power that comes from diminishing our self-will. Surrender your heart, mind, and spirit to God's will, and witness His great and mighty works. Experience the unspeakable joy and full of glory that He promises, and rest in the peace that surpasses all understanding. Allow God to transform every area of your life as you declare, "Nevertheless, not my will, but thine be done." By doing so, you align yourself with His Divine purpose and experience the transformative power of His grace and mercy. With unswerving faith and dedication, you can confidently navigate life's challenges, knowing that God's presence and power sustain you every step of the way.

Consider Jesus in the Garden of Gethsemane. When we comply with God's will, the place we find ourselves may not be to our liking or where we desire to be. Matthew 26:39 (KJV) recounts, "And he went a little farther, and fell on his face, and prayed, saying, O my Father, if it be possible, let this cup pass from me: nevertheless not as I will, but as thou wilt." Even Jesus, in His humanity, faced struggle and submission to the Father's will.

Every test, trial, or experience we encounter is part of God's plan. Romans 8:28 (KJV) reassures us, "And we know that all things work together for good to them that love God, to them who are the called according to his purpose." These events must occur to elevate us to a greater plane. God orchestrates every circumstance to refine us and fulfill His Divine purposes.

We must endure our trials with faith, knowing that God's plans for us are perfect. James 1:2-4 (KJV) encourages us, "My brethren, count it all joy when ye fall into divers temptations; knowing this, that the trying of your faith worketh patience. But let patience have her perfect work, that ye may be perfect and entire, wanting nothing." Trials are opportunities for spiritual growth and maturity, shaping us into the image of Christ.

Trust in God's greater plan, even when the current situation is challenging or distressing. Jeremiah 29:11 (KJV) assures us, "For I know the thoughts that I think toward you, saith the Lord, thoughts of peace, and not of evil, to give you an expected end." God's thoughts towards us are always for our welfare and future hope. His plans are designed to bring us to a place of greater blessing and purpose.

Following Jesus' example in Gethsemane, we learn the power of submission to God's will. Hebrews 5:8-9 (KJV) states, "Though he were a Son, yet learned he obedience by the things which he suffered; and being made perfect, he became the author of eternal salvation unto all them that obey him." Jesus' obedience through suffering became the pathway to salvation for all who believed. Our obedience can lead to great spiritual breakthroughs and victories even in difficult times.

As we continue our journey of purposeful change, let us remember the example of Jesus in the Garden of Gethsemane. Embrace God's timing and purpose, knowing that every trial is part of His Divine plan to elevate us to greater heights. Endure trials with faith, trusting in God's greater plan for our lives. Follow Jesus' example of submission and experience the transformative power of God's grace and mercy. By aligning ourselves with His will, we can confidently navigate life's challenges, knowing that God's presence and power sustain us every step of the way.

Whether walking through the fire, traveling the darkest valley, or climbing the rockiest mountain, we must believe, trust, and pray for God's will to be accomplished. Isaiah 43:2 (KJV) assures us, "When thou passest through the waters, I will be with thee; and through the rivers, they shall not overflow thee: when thou walkest through the fire, thou shalt not be burned; neither shall the flame kindle upon thee." God's presence is with us in every trial, guiding and protecting us.

The strongest position we can be in is complete submission to the Holy Spirit, yielding to His power and control. James 4:7 (KJV) instructs, "Submit yourselves therefore to God. Resist the devil, and he will flee from you." Submission to God is a powerful act of faith, allowing the Holy Spirit to work mightily within us.

Walking through the fire represents facing intense trials and challenges. Daniel 3:25 (KJV) recounts, "He answered and said, Lo, I see four men loose, walking in the midst of the fire, and they have no hurt; and the form of the fourth is like the Son of God." Just as Shadrach, Meshach, and Abednego were protected in the fiery furnace, we, too, are safeguarded by God's presence in our fiery trials.

Traveling the darkest valley symbolizes enduring times of deep sorrow and hardship. Psalm 23:4 (KJV) comforts us, "Yea, though I walk through the valley of the shadow of death, I will fear no evil: for thou art with me; thy rod and thy staff they comfort me." In our darkest moments, God's presence provides comfort and courage.

Climbing the rockiest mountain signifies overcoming seemingly insurmountable obstacles. Philippians 4:13 (KJV) declares, "I can do all things through Christ which strengtheneth me." With Christ's strength, we can conquer any mountain, no matter how formidable it seems.

Prayer is essential in aligning ourselves with God's will. 1 Thessalonians 5:17 (KJV) exhorts us, "Pray without ceasing." Continual prayer keeps us connected to God, allowing His guidance and strength to flow freely into our lives. Through prayer, we submit our desires to His will, trusting His perfect plan.

Yielding to the Holy Spirit means allowing Him to lead and direct our lives. Romans 8:14 (KJV) states, "For as many as are led by the Spirit of God, they are the sons of God." When we yield to the Holy Spirit, we experience His power and wisdom, enabling us to navigate life's challenges with Divine insight.

As we continue our journey of purposeful change, let us believe, trust, and pray for God's will to be accomplished in every trial. Whether walking through the fire, crossing the darkest valley, or climbing the rockiest mountain, trust in God's presence and protection. Embrace the power of complete submission to the Holy Spirit, yielding to His control and guidance. By doing so, you align yourself with God's Divine purpose and experience the transformative power of His grace and mercy. With unwavering faith and dedication, you can confidently navigate life's challenges, knowing that God's presence and power sustain you at every step.

Being fully surrendered to God means being *sold out* to Him. It means that our daily way of living is solely to please God. Psalm 46:10 (KJV) says, "Be still, and know that I am God." This call to stillness invites us to trust fully in God's sovereignty and align our lives with His Divine purpose.

Living to please God should always be our highest priority. Colossians 1:10 (KJV) urges, "That ye might walk worthy of the Lord unto all pleasing, being fruitful in every good work, and increasing in the knowledge of God." When our lives are dedicated to pleasing God, we bear fruit in every good work and grow in understanding His ways.

For our lives to reach their ultimate purpose, we must commit to learning the value of spiritual surrender to God's will. Romans 12:1 (KJV) exhorts, "I beseech you therefore, brethren, by the mercies of God, that ye present your bodies a living sacrifice, holy, acceptable unto God, which is your reasonable service." This act of surrender is no small matter; it involves offering our entire being as a living sacrifice wholly dedicated to God.

To fully surrender, we must embrace God's sovereignty over our lives. Jeremiah 29:11 (KJV) assures us, "For I know the thoughts that I think toward you, saith the Lord, thoughts of peace, and not of evil, to give you an expected end." Trusting that God's plans are good and filled with hope allows us to surrender our fears and uncertainties to Him.

In surrendering to God, we find true peace. Philippians 4:6-7 (KJV) encourages, "Be careful for nothing; but in every thing by prayer and supplication with thanksgiving let your requests be made known unto God. And the peace of God, which passeth all understanding, shall keep your hearts and minds through Christ Jesus." This peace guards our hearts and minds, providing reassurance that God is in control.

Committing to God means living with intention and purpose. Proverbs 3:5-6 (KJV) instructs, "Trust in the Lord with all thine heart; and lean not unto thine own understanding. In all thy ways acknowledge him, and he shall direct thy paths." Acknowledging God in all our ways ensures He guides our steps and directs our paths toward His Divine purpose.

As we continue our journey of purposeful change, let us embrace the essence of full surrender. Be still and recognize the sovereignty of God in every aspect of life. Live each day to please Him, committing to the value of spiritual surrender. Embrace God's sovereignty, find peace in His control, and commit your ways to Him. By doing so, you align yourself with His Divine purpose and experience the transformative power of His grace and mercy. With steadfast faith and dedication, you can confidently navigate life's challenges, knowing that God's presence and power sustain you every step of the way.

We must be cautious of using our humanity as a crutch or an excuse for not giving our all. Romans 3:23 (KJV) reminds us, "For all have sinned, and come short of the glory of God." While it is impossible to be spiritual all the time, we must strive to start each day afresh, giving every ounce of our being to the Lord and allowing Him to handle every situation without our interference.

Lamentations 3:22-23 (KJV) says, "It is of the Lord's mercies that we are not consumed because his compassions fail not. They are new every morning: great is thy faithfulness." Each day is a new opportunity to surrender our lives to God, trusting His mercies and faithfulness. We must strive to start each day with a renewed commitment to live for Him, acknowledging our imperfections but leaning on His strength.

Flesh fails, but God does not. Psalm 73:26 (KJV) proclaims, "My flesh and my heart faileth: but God is the strength of my heart, and my portion for ever." Letting go of self and relinquishing all control to God is extremely challenging because it is human nature to go into self-preservation mode in any situation. However, spiritual maturity involves learning to let go of self and trust God completely.

Proverbs 3:5-6 (KJV) instructs us, "Trust in the Lord with all thine heart; and lean not unto thine own understanding. In all thy ways acknowledge him, and he shall direct thy paths." Complete surrender means acknowledging God's sovereignty in every aspect of our lives and trusting Him to guide us through all circumstances.

Letting go of self comes with spiritual maturity. Galatians 2:20 (KJV) declares, "I am crucified with Christ: nevertheless I live; yet not I, but Christ liveth in me: and the life which I now live in the flesh I live by the faith of the Son of God, who loved me, and gave himself for me." As our faith grows, we learn to live more by the Spirit and less by our understanding and strength.

As we continue our journey of purposeful change, let us be mindful not to use our humanity as an excuse to hold back from giving our all to God. Recognize our imperfections, but strive for daily renewal, surrendering every aspect of our lives to Him. Remember that while our flesh may fail, God never does. Embrace the challenge of complete surrender and trust in His unfailing guidance. By doing so, we align ourselves with His Divine purpose and experience the transformative power of His grace and mercy. With unwavering faith and dedication, we can confidently navigate life's challenges, knowing that God's presence and power sustain us every step of the way.

Let us pray earnestly, "Lord, help us to be who and what You want us to be. Give us strength, boost our faith and hope, and guide us daily. Help us to let go and surrender to You always. Father, may Your will be done, not our own, in Jesus' name."

In our pursuit of God's will, we need His strength. Isaiah 40:31 (KJV) reminds us, "But they that wait upon the Lord shall renew their strength; they shall mount up with wings as eagles; they shall run, and not be weary; and they shall walk, and not faint." Relying on God's strength enables us to overcome obstacles and endure challenges with unwavering faith.

Faith and hope are essential for our spiritual journey. Hebrews 11:1 (KJV) defines faith as "the substance of things hoped for, the evidence of things not seen." Our faith is the foundation of our hope and fuels our perseverance. Romans 15:13 (KJV) further encourages us, "Now the God of hope fill you with all joy and peace in believing, that ye may abound in hope, through the power of the Holy Ghost." With God's help, our faith and hope can flourish.

Guidance from the Lord is crucial for navigating life's complexities. Psalm 32:8 (KJV) promises, "I will instruct thee and teach thee in the way which thou shalt go: I will guide thee with mine eye." Daily seeking His guidance ensures that His wisdom and purpose direct our steps. Proverbs 3:5-6 (KJV) reminds us to trust in the Lord and acknowledge Him in all our ways so He will direct our paths.

True surrender involves letting go of our desires and submitting to God's perfect plan. Luke 22:42 (KJV) records Jesus' ultimate example of surrender: "Father, if thou be willing, remove this cup from me: nevertheless not my will, but thine, be done." Emulating Jesus' submission to the Father's will inevitably lead us to experience God's best for our lives.

Prayer aligns our hearts with God's will. Philippians 4:6-7 (KJV) encourages us, "Be careful for nothing; but in every thing by prayer and supplication with thanksgiving let your requests be made known unto God. And the peace of God, which passeth all understanding, shall keep your hearts and minds through Christ Jesus." Through prayer, we communicate our desires, seek His direction, and find peace in His plans. This is divine peace, which the world can never give to us.

As we continue our journey of purposeful change, let us adopt this prayer of surrender and guidance. Seek God's strength, faith, and hope to navigate each day. Earnestly seek His guidance in all our decisions and actions. Fully surrender to His will, trusting His plans are perfect and far more significant than our own. By doing so, you align yourself with His Divine purpose and experience the transformative power of His grace and mercy. With unwavering faith and dedication, we can confidently traverse life's challenges, knowing that God's presence and power sustain us every step of the way.

God's Word commands us to be strong and courageous, not to be afraid or dismayed. Joshua 1:9 (KJV) declares, "Have not I commanded thee? Be strong and of good courage; be not afraid, neither be thou dismayed: for the Lord thy God is with thee whithersoever thou goest." This

Divine assurance encourages us to face challenges boldly and confidently, knowing that the Lord our God goes before us.

Yielding our will to God's will is a daily effort and application of our heart, mind, and spirit. Romans 12:1-2 (KJV) urges, "I beseech you therefore, brethren, by the mercies of God, that ye present your bodies a living sacrifice, holy, acceptable unto God, which is your reasonable service. And be not conformed to this world: but be ye transformed by the renewing of your mind, that ye may prove what is that good, and acceptable, and perfect, will of God." This daily surrender transforms us and aligns us with God's perfect plan.

If God chooses not to remove us from the fire and pain, we must believe and trust His will, knowing that what transpires is for our greater good and purpose. Romans 8:28 (KJV) reassures us, "And we know that all things work together for good to them that love God, to them who are the called according to his purpose." Even in trials, God's hand is adeptly at work, molding us for His Divine purposes.

In adversity, we find peace in God's presence. Isaiah 41:10 (KJV) comforts us, "Fear thou not; for I am with thee: be not dismayed; for I am thy God: I will strengthen thee; yea,

I will help thee; yea, I will uphold thee with the right hand of my righteousness." This promise assures us of God's ever-present support and strength, even in the darkest times.

Trials and pain often serve as a refining fire, purifying and strengthening our faith. 1 Peter 1:7 (KJV) explains, "That the trial of your faith, being much more precious than of gold that perisheth, though it be tried with fire, might be found unto praise and honour and glory at the appearing of Jesus Christ." Embracing these experiences with trust in God's wisdom refines our character and deepens our relationship with Him.

Yielding to God's will requires a daily commitment. Luke 9:23 (KJV) states, "And he said to them all, If any man will come after me, let him deny himself, and take up his cross daily, and follow me." This daily surrender allows God to lead us, guiding our steps and shaping our destiny according to His perfect will.

As we continue our journey of purposeful change, let us fully embrace the call to be strong and courageous. Yield our will to God's will through daily commitment and trust in His Divine plan. Even if we are not removed from the fire and pain, we believe God's purposes are at work for our greater good. Find peace in His presence, knowing He upholds and strengthens us. By doing so, we align ourselves with His Divine purpose and experience the transformative power of His grace and mercy. With unwavering faith and dedication, we can confidently face life's challenges, knowing that God's presence and power sustain us every step of the way.

It takes significant spiritual strength to say and truly mean the words of complete devotion we speak. May we have a heart eager to surrender and yield to God's will. Philippians 4:13 (KJV) reminds us, "I can do all things through Christ which strengtheneth me." Through Christ's strength, we can genuinely surrender our will to God's.

Having a heart eager to yield to God's will requires daily commitment and intentionality. Proverbs 3:5-6 (KJV) instructs, "Trust in the Lord with all thine heart; and lean not unto thine own understanding. In all thy ways acknowledge him, and he shall direct thy paths." Trusting God means laying aside our desires and embracing His perfect plan for our lives.

Let us pray with hearts fully surrendered: "Lord, nevertheless not my will, but Thine be done. Lord, regardless of my will, Yours be done. Lord, in any event, Your will be accomplished, not mine. Amen and amen." Luke 22:42 (KJV) echoes this sentiment, "Saying, Father, if thou be willing, remove this cup from me: nevertheless not my will, but thine, be done." Jesus' ultimate act of surrender in the Garden of Gethsemane is our ideal model for yielding completely to God's will.

Complete devotion to God's will transforms our lives and aligns us with His Divine purpose. Romans 12:1-2 (KJV) urges, "I beseech you therefore, brethren, by the mercies of God, that ye present your bodies a living sacrifice, holy, acceptable unto God, which is your reasonable service. And be not conformed to this world: but be ye transformed by the renewing of your mind, that ye may prove what is that good, and acceptable, and perfect, will of God." By dedicating ourselves fully to God, we experience His transformative power and live out His perfect will.

Embracing God's sovereignty over our lives requires faith and trust. Jeremiah 29:11 (KJV) assures us, "For I know the thoughts that I think toward you, saith the Lord, thoughts of peace, and not of evil, to give you an expected end." Trusting wholeheartedly that God's plans are good and filled with hope allows us to surrender our fears and uncertainties to Him.

When we surrender to God's will, we experience His peace. Philippians 4:6-7 (KJV) encourages, "Be careful for nothing; but in every thing by prayer and supplication with thanksgiving let your requests be made known unto God. And the peace of God, which passeth all understanding, shall keep your hearts and minds through Christ Jesus." This peace guards our hearts and minds, providing reassurance that God is in control.

As we continue our journey of purposeful change, let us embrace the strength to surrender fully to God's will. Have a heart eager to yield, trusting in His perfect plan. Pray with complete devotion, following the example of Jesus in the Garden of Gethsemane. Embrace God's sovereignty and experience peace by living in His will. By doing so, we align ourselves with His Divine purpose and experience the transformative power of His grace and mercy. With unwavering faith and dedication, we can confidently navigate life's challenges, resting assured that God's presence and power sustain us every step of the way.

Be blessed in in the Lord always!

CHAPTER 7

GOD ON YOU SIDE

UNSHAKEABLE PROTECTION AND PROVISION

"Fear thou not; for I am with thee: be not dismayed; for I am thy God: I will strengthen thee; yea, I will help thee; yea, I will uphold thee with the right hand of my righteousness."(Isaiah 40:10)

We must remember the countless powerful messages delivered by the Holy Spirit. Sometimes, we need a reminder of God's goodness to counteract the spirit of despair the enemy tries to impose upon us. God is changing our circumstances! Romans 8:28 (KJV) assures us, "And we know that all things work together for good to them that love God, to them who are the called according to his purpose."

Despair is a weapon to weaken our faith, but God's power is far greater. Isaiah 41:10 (KJV) encourages us, "Fear thou not; for I am with thee: be not dismayed; for I am thy God: I will strengthen thee; yea, I will help thee; yea, I will uphold thee with the right hand of my righteousness." When we feel overwhelmed, God's presence provides our strength and courage.

God specializes in transforming situations for our benefit. Genesis 50:20 (KJV) tells us, "But as for you, ye thought evil against me; but God meant it unto good, to bring to pass, as it is this day, to save much people alive." Even in adversity, God's sovereignty ensures these trials invariably become opportunities for growth and blessings.

Our safety lies not in the absence of danger but in God's constant presence. Psalm 46:1 (KJV) declares, "God is our refuge and strength, a very present help in trouble." He is our fortress, an unassailable stronghold against any threat. In Him, we find the courage to face our fears.

God Jehovah is our Protector and Defender. Psalm 18:2 (KJV) proclaims, "The Lord is my rock, and my fortress, and my deliverer; my God, my strength, in whom I will trust; my buckler, and the horn of my salvation, and my high tower." This vivid depiction assures us that God is our refuge, shield, and stronghold.

Living under God's favor means experiencing His blessings and guidance in all areas of our lives. Psalm 5:12 (KJV) states, "For thou, Lord, wilt bless the righteous; with favour wilt thou compass him as with a shield." His favor acts as a shield, safeguarding us and leading us toward His divine purposes.

As we constantly seek revival week, remember that God is on our side. Rebuke despair and embrace the assurance that God is turning the tide in our favor. Trust in His presence and power, knowing He is our Protector and Defender. Live under God's favor and witness His blessings unfold in your life. With an abiding faith, we can confidently face any challenge, secure in the knowledge that God's presence sustains us every step of the way. Amen!

Psalm 91 vividly declares God's unwavering protection over His people, reminding us of the security and peace found in His presence. Psalm 91:1-2 (KJV) proclaims, "He that dwelleth in the secret place of the most High shall abide under the shadow of the Almighty. I will say of the Lord, He is my refuge and my fortress: my God; in him will

I trust." Dwelling in His shadow signifies being enveloped in His mighty protection and care.

To dwell in the shadow of the Almighty means to be so close to Him that we are shielded from harm. Psalm 91:4 (KJV) provides a comforting picture: "He shall cover thee with his feathers, and under his wings shalt thou trust: his truth shall be thy shield and buckler." This imagery conveys the intimate care and protection God provides, enveloping us in His love.

God is our refuge and fortress, delivering us from the enemy's snares. Psalm 91:3 (KJV) assures, "Surely he shall deliver thee from the snare of the fowler, and from the noisome pestilence." God's protection renders the enemy's traps powerless.

God's protection extends far beyond the physical, guarding our hearts and minds against fear. Psalm 91:5-6 (KJV) reassures, "Thou shalt not be afraid for the terror by night; nor for the arrow that flieth by day; nor for the pestilence that walketh in darkness; nor for the destruction that wasteth at noonday." His comprehensive protection shields us from both seen and unseen dangers.

God is our shield and buckler, our defense against all forms of evil. Ephesians 6:16 (KJV) echoes this truth, "Above all, taking the shield of faith, wherewith ye shall be able to quench all the fiery darts of the wicked." Our faith in God acts as a shield, deflecting the enemy's attacks.

No wickedness, evil, or plague shall come near our dwelling. Psalm 91:10 (KJV) promises, "There shall no evil befall thee, neither shall any plague come nigh thy dwelling." This assurance of divine protection is a source of immense comfort for all believers.

God gives His angels charge over us to keep us in all our ways. Psalm 91:11 (KJV) proclaims, "For he shall give his angels charge over thee, to keep thee in all thy ways." His angels guide our steps, ensuring our safety.

As we continue our journey, let us rest in the assurance of God's protection, as declared in Psalm 91. Dwell in the shadow of the Almighty, find refuge in His fortress, and trust in His unfailing protection. With God's angels watching over us, we can navigate life's challenges with confidence and peace. Amen!

If the veil of the supernatural world could be pulled back, revealing the evil and wickedness that God shields us from, we would never leave our knees. Ephesians 6:12 (KJV) reveals, "For we wrestle not against flesh and blood, but against principalities, against powers, against the rulers of the darkness of this world, against spiritual wickedness in high places." This unseen battle rages constantly, yet (thankfully!) we are shielded by God's divine protection.

God's hand is ever-present, shielding us from unseen dangers. Psalm 91:1 (KJV) reassures, "He that dwelleth in the secret place of the most High shall abide under the shadow of the Almighty." This secret place underscores our constant dependence on His protection.

Angels are divine warriors assigned to protect us. Hebrews 1:14 (KJV) asks, "Are they not all ministering spirits, sent forth to minister for them who shall be heirs of salvation?" These spirits battle the forces of darkness on our behalf.

Our protection comes from God's vigilance and the tireless ministry of His angels. Psalm 34:7 (KJV) declares, "The angel of the Lord encampeth round about them that fear him, and delivereth them." Knowing this, we can live in peace, assured of His protection.

Understanding the spiritual battles fought on our behalf should drive us to our knees in prayer. Philippians 4:6-7 (KJV) encourages, "Be careful for nothing; but in every thing by prayer and supplication with thanksgiving let your requests be made known unto God. And the peace of God, which passeth all understanding, shall keep your hearts and minds through Christ Jesus."

If we could see the spiritual warfare all around us, our perspective on prayer would transform. 2 Kings 6:17 (KJV) illustrates this reality, "And Elisha prayed, and said, Lord, I pray thee, open his eyes, that he may see. And the Lord opened the eyes of the young man; and he saw: and, behold, the mountain was full of horses and chariots of fire round about Elisha." Like Elisha's servant, we need our spiritual eyes opened to understand God's protection.

Living with the awareness of spiritual battles profoundly changes our approach to life. Ephesians 6:10-11 (KJV) instructs, "Finally, my brethren, be strong in the Lord, and in the power of his might. Put on the whole armour of God, that ye may be able to stand against the wiles of the devil." Clothed in God's armor, we are equipped to face any spiritual challenge.

As we continue our journey, let us acknowledge the unseen battles fought on our behalf. Trust in God's protection and the ministry of His angels. Let this awareness drive us to our knees in prayer. With spiritual eyes opened, we can live confidently, knowing God's presence sustains us every step of the way. Amen!

God's delays are always purposeful. Psalm 23:1-3 (KJV) says, "The Lord is my shepherd; I shall not want. He maketh me to lie down in green pastures: he leadeth me beside the still waters. He restoreth my soul: he leadeth me in the paths of righteousness for his name's sake." Trust His guidance, for He leads us away from unseen dangers.

God's perspective is far above our own. Isaiah 55:8-9 (KJV) reminds us, "For my thoughts are not your thoughts, neither are your ways my ways, saith the Lord. For as the heavens are higher than the earth, so are my ways higher than your ways, and my thoughts than your thoughts." His delays protect us from unseen snares.

God's omniscience assures us that He knows every threat. Psalm 121:7-8 (KJV) declares, "The Lord shall preserve thee from all evil: he shall preserve thy soul. The Lord shall preserve thy going out and thy coming in from this time forth, and even for evermore." His delays are His protection.

Recognize these intervals as precisely what they are: God's merciful intervention. Romans 8:28 (KJV) encourages, "And we know that all things work together for good to them that love God, to them who are the called according to his purpose." These delays align us with His perfect timing.

Trust in His protective delays. Proverbs 3:5-6 (KJV) instructs, "Trust in the Lord with all thine heart; and lean not unto thine own understanding. In all thy ways acknowledge him, and he shall direct thy paths." By surrendering impatience, we allow Him to guide us safely.

Embrace God's timing. Ecclesiastes 3:1 (KJV) says, "To every thing there is a season, and a time to every purpose under the heaven." Each delay is part of His orchestration.

As we continue our journey, let us embrace God's timing with gratitude. Recognize delays as His protection. Appreciate His view, knowing He leads us with wisdom. By surrendering to His timing, we align with His purpose. With unwavering faith, we can navigate life's challenges, knowing God's presence sustains us every step of the way. Amen!

When we face severe attacks, the key is to remember that God sees the deception. Psalm 34:19 (KJV) reminds, "Many are the afflictions of the righteous: but the Lord delivereth him out of them all." God's omniscient gaze penetrates the darkness.

God's intervention is both powerful and precise. Psalm 18:16-17 (KJV) illustrates this, "He sent from above, he took me, he drew me out of many waters. He delivered me from my strong enemy, and from them which hated me: for they were too strong for me." This rescue is a testament to His commitment.

God's protection is always upon us. Isaiah 41:10 (KJV) assures, "Fear thou not; for I am with thee: be not dismayed; for I am thy God: I will strengthen thee; yea, I will help thee; yea, I will uphold thee with the right hand of my righteousness." This promise reminds us of His unlimited capability.

Standing firm in God's will means being steadfast. Ephesians 6:13 (KJV) encourages, "Wherefore take unto you the whole armour of God, that ye may be able to withstand in the evil day, and having done all, to stand." Clothed in God's armor, we withstand the enemy's attacks.

God's timing is perfect. Psalm 40:1-2 (KJV) declares, "I waited patiently for the Lord; and he inclined unto me, and heard my cry. He brought me up also out of an horrible pit, out of the miry clay, and set my feet upon a rock, and established my goings." Trusting His timing ensures our rescue.

Having faith in God's deliverance strengthens us. Hebrews 11:6 (KJV) states, "But without faith it is impossible to please him: for he that cometh to God must believe that he is, and that he is a rewarder of them that diligently seek him." Diligent pursuit brings His interventions.

As we continue our journey, let us remain steadfast in the knowledge that God foresees every threat. Trust in His powerful hand to deliver us. Stand firm, clothed in His armor, and wait for His timing. We can navigate life's challenges with unwavering faith, knowing God's presence sustains us. Amen!

God transforms our burdens into blessings. Romans 8:28 (KJV) declares, "And we know that all things work together for good to them that love God, to them who are the called according to his purpose." Yes, even heavy burdens become channels of God's grace.

He turns our hurts into hopes. Jeremiah 29:11 (KJV) assures, "For I know the thoughts that I think toward you, saith the Lord, thoughts of peace, and not of evil, to give you an expected end." Pains and trials are part of God's plan for peace.

God's ability to bring good out of evil testifies to His grace. 2 Corinthians 12:9 (KJV) says, "And he said unto me, My grace is sufficient for thee: for my strength is made perfect in weakness." In weakness, God's grace shines brightest.

With God by our side, we fear no evil. Psalm 27:1 (KJV) proclaims, "The Lord is my light and my salvation; whom shall I fear? the Lord is the strength of my life; of whom shall I be afraid?" This assurance empowers us.

Living in the reality of God's power means embracing His ability to turn negatives into opportunities. Genesis 50:20 (KJV) illustrates, "But as for you, ye thought evil against me; but God meant it unto good, to bring to pass, as it is this day, to save much people alive." God uses evil for our good.

As we continue our journey, let us celebrate God's power to transform harm into blessings. Praise Him for turning burdens into blessings and hurts into hopes. Embrace His grace, knowing His strength is made perfect in weakness. Live fearlessly, trusting in God's protection. With resolute faith, we can navigate life's challenges, assured God's presence sustains us. Amen!

God does not stop every storm, for through challenges, we develop spiritually. James 1:2-4 (KJV) encourages, "My brethren, count it all joy when ye fall into divers temptations; knowing this, that the trying of your faith worketh patience. But let patience have her perfect work, that ye may be perfect and entire, wanting nothing." Trials build up our faith muscles.

Without trials, we would never develop spiritual strength. Romans 5:3-4 (KJV) states, "And not only so, but we glory in tribulations also: knowing that tribulation worketh patience; and patience, experience; and experience, hope." Each difficulty develops endurance and character.

God does not leave us alone in storms. He rides out the storms with us. Isaiah 41:10 (KJV) reassures, "Fear thou not; for I am with thee: be not dismayed; for I am thy God: I will strengthen thee; yea, I will help thee; yea, I will uphold thee with the right hand of my righteousness." His presence is our anchor.

In weakness, God's strength sustains us. 2 Corinthians 12:9 (KJV) affirms, "And he said unto me, My grace is sufficient for thee: for my strength is made perfect in weakness." Our complete dependence on His strength transforms trials into testimonies.

We must discern the Holy Spirit's guidance. John 16:13 (KJV) promises, "Howbeit when he, the Spirit of truth, is come, he will guide you into all truth: for he shall not speak of himself; but whatsoever he shall hear, that shall he speak: and he will shew you things to come." The Holy Spirit is our guide.

Embracing trials as opportunities for growth changes our perspective. Hebrews 12:11 (KJV) reminds, "Now no chastening for the present seemeth to be joyous, but grievous: nevertheless afterward it yieldeth the peaceable fruit of righteousness unto them which are exercised thereby." Through storms, God cultivates righteousness.

As we continue our journey, let us welcome storms as opportunities for growth. Trust that God rides out storms with us. Pay attention to the Holy Spirit's guidance. Strengthen your faith muscles and grow in the Lord. We can navigate life's challenges with unwavering faith, knowing God's presence sustains us. Amen!

The Holy Spirit emphasized the importance of recognizing and respecting closed doors. Revelation 3:7 (KJV) reminds, "And to the angel of the church in Philadelphia writes; These things saith he that is holy, he that is true, he that hath the key of David, he that openeth, and no man shutteth; and shutteth, and no man openeth." Closed doors are purposeful.

We must stop trying to open closed doors. Proverbs 19:21 (KJV) teaches, "There are many devices in a man's heart; nevertheless the counsel of the Lord, that shall stand." Trust His decisions.

When God says no, it is often for our protection. Psalm 121:7-8 (KJV) assures, "The Lord shall preserve thee from all evil: he shall preserve thy soul. The Lord shall preserve thy going out and thy coming in from this time forth, and even for evermore." His "no" is a safeguard.

We can become self-destructive, pursuing what God has closed off. Isaiah 55:8-9 (KJV) reminds us, "For my thoughts are not your thoughts, neither are your ways my ways, saith the Lord. For as the heavens are higher than the earth, so are my ways higher than your ways, and my thoughts than your thoughts." Trusting His wisdom prevents detriment.

Thank God for His insights and safeguards. Psalm 32:8 (KJV) promises, "I will instruct thee and teach thee in the way which thou shalt go: I will guide thee with mine eye." His guidance is a precious gift.

Embracing God's wisdom means accepting His decisions. Proverbs 3:5-6 (KJV) instructs, "Trust in the Lord with all thine heart; and lean not unto thine own understanding. In all thy ways acknowledge him, and he shall direct thy paths." Trusting His direction ensures safety.

As we continue our journey, let us trust God's wisdom when He closes doors. Recognize His actions are for our growth. By embracing His guidance, we can avoid self-destructive behaviors. We can navigate life's challenges with unwavering faith, knowing God's presence sustains us. Amen!

We must focus on our mighty Lord and Savior. Hebrews 12:2 encourages, "Looking unto Jesus the author and finisher of our faith; who for the joy that was set before him endured the cross, despising the shame, and is set down at the right hand of the throne of God." By focusing on Jesus, we find strength and direction.

We must put on our spiritual armor. Ephesians 6:11 instructs, "Put on the whole armour of God, that ye may be able to stand against the wiles of the devil." This armor is indispensable for our protection.

The belt of truth grounds us in God's Word. John 8:32 states, "And ye shall know the truth, and the truth shall make you free." Truth provides stability.

The breastplate of righteousness protects our hearts. Proverbs 4:23 advises, "Keep thy heart with all diligence; for out of it are the issues of life." Righteousness guards our hearts.

The gospel shoes of peace enable us to stand firm. Romans 10:15 proclaims, "And how shall they preach, except they be sent? as it is written, How beautiful are the feet of them that preach the gospel of peace, and bring glad tidings of good things!" Peace steadies our steps.

The shield of faith extinguishes the enemy's darts. Hebrews 11:6 asserts, "But without faith it is impossible to please him: for he that cometh to God must believe that he is, and that he is a rewarder of them that diligently seek him." Faith tenaciously repels attacks.

The helmet of salvation protects our minds. 1 Thessalonians 5:8 states, "But let us, who are of the day, be sober, putting on the breastplate of faith and love; and for an helmet, the hope of salvation." Salvation assures our destiny.

The sword of the Spirit is the Word of God and is our offensive weapon. Hebrews 4:12 declares, "For the word of God is quick, and powerful, and sharper than any two-edged sword, piercing even to the dividing asunder of soul and spirit, and of the joints and marrow, and is a discerner of the thoughts and intents of the heart." God's Word empowers us.

We must keep our armor on, for the enemy will slip through small cracks. Ephesians 6:13 emphasizes, "Wherefore take unto you the whole armour of God, that ye may be able to withstand in the evil day, and having done all, to stand." Ensure every piece is securely worn.

As we continue our journey, let us focus on our mighty Lord and Savior. Put on the whole armor of God. The belt of truth, the breastplate of righteousness, the gospel shoes of peace, the shield of faith, the helmet of salvation, and the sword of the Spirit are all essential. Trust in God's provision, stand firm, and confidently navigate life's challenges, knowing God's presence sustains us. Amen!

We must stand steadfast on God's promises. Psalm 34:7 (KJV) declares, "The angel of the Lord encampeth round about them that fear him, and delivereth them." This protection assures us that we are always guarded.

The enemy will oppose us, but we must remember Job's profound words. Job 19:25 (KJV) proclaims, "For I know that my redeemer liveth, and that he shall stand at the latter day upon the earth." Job's unwavering faith is a powerful example.

The enemy will battle us, but Satan cannot cross the bloodline. Revelation 12:11 (KJV) reminds us, "And they overcame him by the blood of the Lamb, and by the word of their testimony; and they loved not their lives unto the death." The blood of Jesus is our victory.

God's protection is unfailing. Psalm 91:11 (KJV) reassures, "For he shall give his angels charge over thee, to keep thee in all thy ways." With His angels, we can face any challenge.

Standing firm in faith means trusting God's promises. Ephesians 6:16 (KJV) instructs, "Above all, taking the shield of faith, wherewith ye shall be able to quench all the fiery darts of the wicked." Our faith acts as a highly dependable shield.

Declare victory in Christ, as Job did. 1 Corinthians 15:57 (KJV) affirms, "But thanks be to God, which giveth us the victory through our Lord Jesus Christ." Through Jesus, we have victory.

As we continue our journey, let us stand steadfast on God's promises. Face the enemy with Job's powerful faith, declaring our Redeemer lives. Remember that Satan cannot cross the bloodline. Stand firm in faith, trust God's promises, and declare victory in Christ. We can navigate life's challenges with unwavering faith, knowing God's presence sustains us. Amen!

We come against Satan and his demons, commanding wicked spirits to be uprooted and bound in Jesus' name. Matthew 18:18 (KJV) assures, "Verily I say unto you, Whatsoever ye shall bind on earth shall be bound in heaven: and whatsoever ye shall loose on earth shall be loosed in heaven." We stand firm against darkness.

We bind sickness and disease and lose the Holy Spirit in Jesus' name. Mark 16:17-18 (KJV) declares, "And these signs shall follow them that believe; In my name shall they cast out devils; they shall speak with new tongues; They shall take up serpents; and if they drink any deadly thing, it shall not hurt them; they shall lay hands on the sick, and they shall recover." Exercise this authority to break affliction.

God, heighten our discernment, we pray. Proverbs 2:3-5 (KJV) encourages, "Yea, if thou criest after knowledge, and liftest up thy voice for understanding; If thou seekest her as silver, and searchest for her as for hid treasures; Then shalt thou understand the fear of the Lord, and find the knowledge of God." Grant understanding to make knowledgeable judgments.

God, help us be bold and breathe through fear. Isaiah 43:2 (KJV) promises, "When thou passest through the waters, I will be with thee; and through the rivers, they shall not overflow thee: when thou walkest through the fire, thou shalt not be burned; neither shall the flame kindle upon thee." Your presence gives us courage.

We command victory in Jesus' name. Ephesians 6:10-11 (KJV) instructs, "Finally, my brethren, be strong in the Lord, and in the power of his might. Put on the whole armour of God, that ye may be able to stand against the wiles of the devil." Clothed in God's armor, we declare triumph.

As we continue our journey, let us boldly confront darkness with Jesus' authority. Bind the enemy's works and loose the Holy Spirit's power. Pray for discernment and understanding. Walk boldly through life's fires with God's strength. Command victory in Jesus' name, knowing God's presence sustains us. Amen!

Thank You, God, for Your protection! Thank You for turning things around for our good. Romans 8:28 (KJV) assures, "And we know that all things work together for good to them that love God, to them who are the called according to his purpose." This promise is a cornerstone of our faith.

God's protection is unceasing. Psalm 91:4 (KJV) declares, "He shall cover thee with his feathers, and under his wings shalt thou trust: his truth shall be thy shield and buckler." Like a loving parent, our Father shields us from harm.

God transforms challenging situations for our benefit. Genesis 50:20 (KJV) illustrates, "But as for you, ye thought evil against me; but God meant it unto good, to bring to pass, as it is this day, to save much people alive." God turns destruction into testimony.

In acknowledging God's sovereignty, we find peace. Proverbs 3:5-6 (KJV) instructs, "Trust in the Lord with all thine heart; and lean not unto thine own understanding. In all thy ways acknowledge him, and he shall direct thy paths." Trusting His wisdom, we boldly navigate life's uncertainties with confidence.

Gratitude for God's faithfulness deepens our relationship. Lamentations 3:22-23 (KJV) reminds us, "It is of the Lord's mercies that we are not consumed, because his compassions fail not. They are new every morning: great is thy faithfulness." Every day presents us with a brand-new opportunity to witness His mercy.

Living in the assurance of God's goodness completely transforms our outlook. Psalm 27:13 (KJV) declares, "I had fainted, unless I had believed to see the goodness of the Lord in the land of the living." Focusing on His goodness strengthens us.

As we continue our journey, let us remain grateful for God's protection and transformation. Thank Him for working all things for our good. Trust His sovereignty. Live in His goodness, knowing His presence sustains us. We can navigate life's challenges with gratitude and faith, praising God for His protection and orchestration. Amen!

Be blessed in the Lord always!

CHAPTER 8

A GUARDED HEART

PROTECTED BY THE SPIRIT OF GOD

"And the peace of God, which passeth all understanding, shall keep your hearts and minds through Christ Jesus."(Philippians 4:7)

Guarding our hearts should be of the utmost importance. Proverbs 4:23 (KJV), Scripture emphasizes this: "Keep thy heart with all diligence; for out of it are the issues of life." Our heart is the core of both our physical and spiritual being, the source of our thoughts, actions, and emotions. This underscores the critical nature of protecting our hearts, ensuring they remain pure and aligned with God's will.

The human heart is either a temple for God or a stronghold for Satan; there is absolutely no middle ground. 2 Corinthians 6:14 (KJV) states, "Be ye not unequally yoked together with unbelievers: for what fellowship hath righteousness with unrighteousness? and what communion hath light with darkness?" Light and darkness cannot coexist, just as God cannot dwell where sin prevails. Therefore, our hearts must be wholly devoted to Him. When our hearts become the dwelling place of the Holy Spirit, we become vessels of His grace, love, and power.

Guarding our hearts requires vigilance regarding what we allow to influence our inner being. Proverbs 23:7 (KJV) says, "For as he thinketh in his heart, so is he." Our thoughts shape our identity and actions. Hence, we must be mindful of our thoughts, words, and deeds, ensuring they align with God's will. The condition of our heart directly affects our spiritual health and relationship with God, influencing every decision and interaction.

The purity of our hearts is crucial for our spiritual health and relationship with God. Matthew 5:8 (KJV) promises, "Blessed are the pure in heart: for they shall see God." A pure heart, free from sin's contamination, aligns with God's righteousness. Through a pure heart, we can experience the fullness of God's presence and blessings.

Purity of the heart is not merely the absence of sin but the embodiment of God's holiness, transforming our thoughts, desires, and actions.

The heart is a battleground where good and evil vie for control. Jeremiah 17:9 (KJV) warns, "The heart is deceitful above all things, and desperately wicked: who can know it?" This highlights the need to guard our hearts against Satan's deceit and wickedness. By filling our hearts with God's Word and surrounding ourselves with His truth, we fortify ourselves against the enemy's attacks. The battle for our hearts requires constant vigilance, prayer, and reliance on the Holy Spirit's guidance.

The Holy Spirit plays a crucial role in guarding our hearts. John 14:26 (KJV) says, "But the Comforter, which is the Holy Ghost, whom the Father will send in my name, he shall teach you all things, and bring all things to your remembrance, whatsoever I have said unto you." The Holy Spirit guides us in truth, convicts us of sin, and helps us keep our hearts pure and focused on God. He empowers us to live righteously and strengthens us against temptation, providing the discernment needed for victory in life's spiritual battles.

To guard our hearts effectively, we must be intentional in our spiritual practices:

Prayer: Regular communication with God keeps our hearts aligned with His will. Philippians 4:6-7 (KJV) instructs, "Be careful for nothing; but in every thing by prayer and supplication with thanksgiving let your requests be made known unto God. And the peace of God, which passeth all understanding, shall keep your hearts and minds through Christ Jesus." Prayer connects us to God's heart and aligns our desires with His.

Bible Study: Immersing ourselves in Scripture renews our minds and purifies our hearts. Psalm 119:11 (KJV) declares, "Thy word have I hid in mine heart, that I might not sin against thee." Studying God's Word fills our hearts with His truth, equipping us to resist the enemy's lies and deceptions.

Worship: Genuine worship focuses our hearts on God's greatness and goodness. John 4:24 (KJV) states, "God is a Spirit: and they that worship him must worship him in spirit and in truth." Worship shifts our focus from our malleable circumstances to God's unchanging nature, fostering gratitude and reverence.

Fellowship: Surrounding ourselves with fellow believers strengthens our resolve and provides accountability. Hebrews 10:24-25 (KJV) encourages, "And let us consider one another to provoke unto love and to good works: Not forsaking the assembling of ourselves together, as the manner of some is; but exhorting one another: and so much the more, as ye see the day approaching." Fellowship helps us stay encouraged and accountable in our walk with Christ.

Obedience: Living in obedience to God's commands protects our hearts from sin's influence. 1 Samuel 15:22 (KJV) reminds us, "Hath the Lord as great delight in burnt offerings and sacrifices, as in obeying the voice of the Lord? Behold, to obey is better than sacrifice, and to hearken than the fat of rams." Obedience is an act of worship that demonstrates our love and commitment to God, keeping our hearts aligned with His will.

As we continue this journey guarding our hearts, let us remember its vital importance. Our hearts are the wellspring of our lives, and everything we do flows from them. By dedicating our hearts wholly to God, we ensure they remain pure, protected, and aligned with His Divine purpose. With the Holy Spirit's guidance and a commitment to spiritual discipline, we can guard our hearts against all forms of evil, keeping them sanctuaries of God's presence and power. Let us be vigilant, intentional, and steadfast in pursuing a guarded heart, fully devoted to our Lord and Savior. Amen!

The heart of man is born into sin, and from it come evil thoughts, making us unclean. Jeremiah 17:9 (KJV) reveals, "The heart is deceitful above all things, and desperately wicked: who can know it?" This inherent wickedness drives sinful behaviors and thoughts that separate us from God. Recognizing the depravity of the human heart underscores the necessity of spiritual renewal and vigilance in protecting it from the enemy's influence.

We must give our hearts to God and be born again. John 3:3 (KJV) declares, "Jesus answered and said unto him, Verily, verily, I say unto thee, except a man be born again, he cannot see the kingdom of God." This rebirth is essential for cleansing our hearts and transforming our lives. When we surrender our hearts to God, He creates in us a new heart, one aligned with His will and capable of righteous living.

After being born again, protecting and guarding our hearts from the enemy's infiltration is crucial. 1 Peter 5:8 (KJV) warns, "Be sober, be vigilant; because your adversary the devil, as a roaring lion, walketh about, seeking whom he may devour." The enemy constantly seeks opportunities to infiltrate our hearts and lead us astray. Therefore, we must remain vigilant, guarding our hearts with all diligence.

Guarding our hearts involves continuous surrender to God. Proverbs 4:23 (KJV) reminds us, "Keep thy heart with all diligence; for out of it are the issues of life." This means daily committing our hearts to God, seeking His guidance, and allowing His Word to shape our thoughts and actions. Through continuous surrender, we fortify our hearts against the enemy's attacks and remain steadfast in our faith.

The Holy Spirit empowers us to guard our hearts effectively. Galatians 5:16 (KJV) encourages, "This I say then, Walk in the Spirit, and ye shall not fulfil the lust of the flesh." By walking in the Spirit, we can resist temptations and maintain a pure heart. The Holy Spirit provides the strength and discernment to navigate daily spiritual battles.

Engaging in spiritual disciplines is vital for guarding our hearts. These disciplines include prayer, Bible study, worship, fellowship, and obedience. Philippians 4:6-7 (KJV) states, "Be careful for nothing; but in every thing by prayer and supplication with thanksgiving let your requests be made known unto God. And the peace of God, which passeth all understanding, shall keep your hearts and minds through Christ Jesus." Practicing these disciplines keeps our hearts aligned with God's will and protected from the enemy's schemes.

As we continue our journey of purposeful change, let us recognize the inherent sinfulness of the human heart and the necessity of being born again. By surrendering our hearts to God and continuously guarding them through spiritual disciplines and the power of the Holy Spirit, we can protect ourselves from the enemy's wicked influence. Let us remain vigilant, diligent, and steadfast in our commitment to God, ensuring our hearts remain pure, protected, and aligned with His Divine purpose. With unflinching faith and determination, we can confidently navigate life's challenges, assured that God's presence and power sustain us every step of the way. Amen!

When we give our heart to God, it signifies the beginning of a new life, a new purpose, and a renewed sense of self. 2 Corinthians 5:17 (KJV) proclaims, "Therefore if any man be in Christ, he is a new creature: old things are passed away; behold, all things are become new." This transformation from the old self to a new creation in Christ is the cornerstone of our spiritual journey.

Embracing this new life involves a radical change from who we once were. Ephesians 4:22-24 (KJV) instructs, "That ye put off concerning the former conversation the old man, which is corrupt according to the deceitful lusts; and be renewed in the spirit of your mind; and that ye put on the new man, which after God is created in righteousness and true holiness." This renewal is not merely a superficial change but a full transformation that affects every aspect of our being.

To be pure-hearted is to have an honest and sincere heart free from bitterness, malice, betrayal, or evil intent. Psalm 51:10 (KJV) prays, "Create in me a clean heart, O God; and renew a right spirit within me." A pure heart seeks God earnestly and strives to reflect His love and righteousness in all things.

Honesty and sincerity are fundamental qualities of a pure heart. Proverbs 12:22 (KJV) says, "Lying lips are abomination to the Lord: but they that deal truly are his delight." Living with integrity and truthfulness honors God and fosters trust and respect in our relationships with others.

A heart free from bitterness and malice is essential for spiritual growth and harmony. Ephesians 4:31-32 (KJV) exhorts, "Let all bitterness, and wrath, and anger, and clamor, and evil speaking, be put away from you, with all malice: and be ye kind one to another, tenderhearted, forgiving one another, even as God for Christ's sake hath forgiven you." Forgiveness and kindness are hallmarks of a heart transformed by God's grace.

A pure heart rejects betrayal and evil intent, choosing instead to embody love and righteousness. Romans 12:9 (KJV) commands, "Let love be without dissimulation. Abhor that which is evil; cleave to that which is good." By adhering to these principles, we demonstrate the transformative power of God's love in our lives.

Living out our new purpose means continually seeking God's will and striving to glorify Him in all we do. Colossians 3:23-24 (KJV) encourages, "And whatsoever ye do, do it heartily, as to the Lord, and not unto men; knowing that of the Lord ye shall receive the reward of the inheritance: for ye serve the Lord Christ." Motivated by a pure heart, our actions should reflect our commitment to serving God and advancing His kingdom.

As we continue our journey of purposeful change, let us embrace the new life, purpose, and sense of self that comes from giving our hearts to God. Strive to be pure-hearted, honest, and sincere, free from bitterness, malice, betrayal, and evil intent. Live out this transformation by seeking God's will and glorifying Him. With a heart renewed by God's grace and guided by the Holy Spirit, we can confidently navigate life's challenges, assured that His presence and power sustain us every step. Amen!

What comes out of the mouth reflects the heart's true state. Every heart will ultimately reveal its nature, whether pure or defiled. We must exercise extreme caution when justifying our actions based on our fleshly minds, as what might seem acceptable to us is not always pleasing to God. No sin is justified in His eyes.

If we harbor anything in our hearts that is not true, honest, just, pure, lovely, or of good report, we face serious spiritual problems. God's Word declares, "There is a generation that are pure in their own eyes and yet are not washed from their filthiness." This warning serves as a call for deep self-examination and repentance.

We must continually assess our hearts and strive for purity and righteousness. We must seek God's help in this journey, acknowledging our need for His guidance and grace. By aligning our hearts with His Divine standards, we can aspire to live lives that truly honor and reflect His holiness.

The enemy wages war over the unseen aspects of our lives. He is not interested in our money or material possessions; his targets are far more consequential. He seeks to control our minds, influence our attitudes, undermine our faith, disturb our peace, and ultimately corrupt our hearts. He aims to attack the core of our being, the essence of what makes us function.

Alarmingly, the enemy is succeeding in driving a wedge within the Body of Christ. This division weakens our collective strength and undermines our mission. We must recognize this spiritual warfare and respond with vigilance and unity. The Church needs a refresher course on what it means to have the love of God in our hearts. This love is not merely a feeling but a transformative force that shapes our actions, attitudes, and relationships. It calls us to live in harmony, extend grace, and demonstrate genuine care for one another.

We must reaffirm our commitment to embodying God's love in these challenging times. Let us strive to protect our minds and hearts, maintain our faith and peace, and support each other in the spiritual battle we face. By doing so, we can resist the enemy's schemes and uphold the true essence of our faith.

God's Word assures us, "And the peace of God, which passeth all understanding, shall keep your hearts and minds through Christ Jesus" (Philippians 4:7, KJV). This Divine peace is a loving gift, a protective shield for our hearts and minds, offering tranquility beyond human comprehension.

We must introspect: Do we truly possess this peace of God, or has the devil slyly infiltrated our lives and stolen it? The enemy's tactics are insidious, disrupting our inner harmony and instilling turmoil within our souls.

To maintain this peace, we must be vigilant and steadfast in our faith. This necessitates continually seeking God's presence, immersing ourselves in His Word, and cultivating a powerful prayer life. By doing so, we fortify our hearts and minds against the enemy's schemes, ensuring that God's peace remains our unyielding stronghold.

Let us reclaim and cherish this Divine peace, allowing it to reign supreme. In the face of chaos and uncertainty, God's peace will anchor us, guiding us through every challenge and trial. By holding fast to this promise, we can experience the fullness of life in Christ Jesus, confident and secure in His unending love and grace.

May we always strive to guard this precious peace, understanding that it is not merely a fleeting emotion but a Divine assurance, a testament to our faith in God's unalterable promises.

In an ideal world, we might be able to remain in perfect peace, but the reality of life presents its challenges. Satan, described in Scripture as one who comes "to steal, and to kill, and to destroy" (John 10:10, KJV), is constantly on the prowl, seeking to devour us. He uses his schemes and devices to sow tares among the brethren, planting just one seed of wickedness and deceit, then retreating into the shadows to watch it grow into a mighty mountain of darkness. This darkness can be so overwhelming that God's people struggle to see beyond it.

However, it is also possible that our inability to see past these mountains stems from our self-righteousness. Sometimes, we are blinded by our pride, failing to recognize our need for God's grace and guidance. We must remember that our battle is not against flesh and blood but against spiritual wickedness in high places (Ephesians 6:12, KJV).

To combat this, we must arm ourselves with God's armor: truth, righteousness, the gospel of peace, faith, salvation, and the Word of God. Only by doing so can we stand firm against the enemy's attacks and clear the darkness that clouds our vision.

Let us be vigilant in our spiritual walk, acknowledging our dependence on God's strength and wisdom. By humbling ourselves and seeking His guidance, we can overcome the enemy's schemes and maintain the peace that surpasses all understanding. As we do so, we illuminate the path before us, allowing God's light to dispel the darkness and guide us through life's challenges.

In this ongoing spiritual warfare, may we continually seek God's protection and embody His love and grace, ensuring our hearts remain steadfast and our vision clear. By doing so, we can rise above the enemy's deceptions and live in the fullness of God's peace and truth.

God, help the lies of the enemy to dissolve from our eyes! We must guard our hearts against these toxic and consuming poisons. The enemy's deceptions are pervasive, seeking to infiltrate our thoughts and actions, but we must remain vigilant in our spiritual walk.

To protect ourselves, we must be diligent and intentional in our efforts to live holy lives. Scripture reminds us, "Keep thy heart with all diligence; for out of it are the issues of life" (Proverbs 4:23, KJV). This verse underscores the importance of safeguarding our hearts, as it is the wellspring of our actions and attitudes.

Living a holy life requires conscious effort and dedication. We must consistently seek God's guidance, immerse ourselves in His Word, and cultivate a prayerful relationship. Doing so strengthens our spiritual defenses and ensures our hearts remain pure and aligned with His will.

Let us encourage one another to stay vigilant and committed in this journey. As the Body of Christ, we must support and uplift each other, reminding ourselves of our high calling in Christ Jesus. "But as he which hath called you is holy, so be ye holy in all manner of conversation" (1 Peter 1:15, KJV).

Through God's grace and our steadfast effort, we can overcome the enemy's lies and live lives that reflect His holiness. May we strive daily to embody the purity and righteousness that God desires, keeping our hearts guarded and our spirits strong.

By remaining vigilant and concerted in our efforts to live holy, we can resist the enemy's schemes and walk in the fullness of God's truth and peace. Let us press on with determination, knowing that our efforts are not in vain and that God's strength is made perfect in our weakness.

Guarding the heart requires careful balance. We must shield and protect it from sin and the enemy, but we must also be careful not to shut it down from those we love. Our hearts are the wellspring of life, and while they need protection, they also need to remain open to love and connection.

Opening our hearts and having the true love of God inside brings our greatest joy. This Divine love, which surpasses all understanding, fills us with peace and happiness. It enables us to connect deeply with others and reflects God's immense love for us. "And above all things have fervent charity among yourselves: for charity shall cover the multitude of sins" (1 Peter 4:8, KJV).

Wisdom is our greatest tool in this delicate task. The Bible reminds us, "Wisdom is the principal thing; therefore get wisdom: and with all thy getting get understanding" (Proverbs 4:7, KJV). Wisdom helps us discern when to guard our hearts and when to open them, guiding us to make choices that honor God and nurture our relationships.

Let us seek God's wisdom in everything, allowing it to direct our actions and decisions. By doing so, we can effectively guard our hearts from harm while embracing the fullness of God's love and sharing it with others. This balance is essential for living a life that glorifies God and brings true joy to our hearts.

May we always strive to maintain this balance, protecting our hearts from the enemy's attacks while keeping them open to the love and joy that God intends for us. By relying on God's wisdom, we can navigate this delicate balance and experience the abundant life He promises.

Our hearts are precious to God. He treasures them deeply and desires them to be pure and aligned with His Divine will. While He will never force or override our free will, He clearly instructs us in His Word to "keep thy heart with all diligence; for out of it are the issues of life" (Proverbs 4:23, KJV). This directive highlights our hearts' crucial role in determining the course of our lives.

God understands our heart's impact on our actions, thoughts, and overall direction. By diligently guarding our hearts, we ensure they remain a source of goodness, truth, and love. This requires us to be vigilant against negative influences and sin while nurturing our hearts with God's Word, prayer, and fellowship with other believers.

When we guard our hearts with diligence, we open ourselves to the transformative power of God's love. This Divine love protects us and empowers us to live righteously and joyfully. "Thy word have I hid in mine heart, that I might not sin against thee" (Psalm 119:11, KJV). By internalizing God's Word, we fortify our hearts against the enemy's schemes and ensure that our lives reflect His glory.

Let us commit to guarding our hearts with all diligence. By doing so, we align ourselves with God's will and secure a path to abundant life and eternal joy. In this endeavor, we are never alone, for God is with us, guiding and strengthening us every step of the way.

May we recognize the preciousness of our heart to God and take every measure to protect and nurture it. In doing so, we fulfill His command and experience the fullness of life He promises.

Our eyes and ears are the gateways to our hearts. What we see and watch, the words and conversations we hear, all filter into our hearts and take residence. Therefore, we must diligently protect and guard our hearts, as Satan tenaciously aims to corrupt and defile them.

The enemy is sly, much like a snake, and will slither in quickly if given the opportunity. He seeks to desecrate and defile our hearts. We must be cautious that the enemy does not persuade us to justify our sins or convince us that we are right and justified in our feelings while everyone else is wrong. As the Bible warns, "The heart is deceitful above all things, and desperately wicked: who can know it?" (Jeremiah 17:9, KJV). Unrepented sin will separate us from God, and vigilance is crucial.

Jesus is coming, and there are no do-overs. We must ensure that we can speak to each other, lift one another up, encourage, and have fellowship within our churches and with our brothers and sisters in Christ. If we cannot do this, something is seriously wrong. "For if ye forgive men their trespasses, your heavenly Father will also forgive you: But if ye forgive not men their trespasses, neither will your Father forgive your trespasses" (Matthew 6:14-15, KJV).

One person's problem can quickly grow into a problem for many. Therefore, we must address issues promptly and bring them under the blood of Christ. As Scripture advises, "Keep thy heart with all diligence; for out of it are the issues of life" (Proverbs 4:23, KJV). Shields up! Guard our hearts!

Maintaining our spiritual defenses is crucial in these times. Ensuring our hearts remain pure and aligned with God's will protects us from the enemy's vile schemes and preserves our connection with God, preparing us for the return of our Savior.

Be blessed in the Lord always!

CHAPTER 9

A DARK PAST IS PAST

REDEMPTION AND NEWNESS OF LIFE

"Therefore if any man be in Christ, he is a new creature: old things are passed away; behold, all things are become new."
(2 Corinthians 5:17)

As I sought the guidance of the Holy Spirit on what to share about my dark past, He brought to mind the story of Rahab, a woman whose history was marred by sin yet transformed into a testament of divine grace and strength. Rahab's journey from darkness to redemption serves as a powerful reminder of God's ability to use anyone, regardless of their past, for His glorious purposes.

In the Book of Joshua, Rahab's story unfolds as she courageously hides the Israelite spies, an act that leads to her and her family's salvation during the fall of Jericho. Despite her initial life as a harlot, Rahab becomes a significant figure in the lineage of Jesus Christ, illustrating the transformative power of faith and redemption. The scripture says, "And Joshua saved Rahab the harlot alive, and her father's household, and all that she had; and she dwelleth in Israel even unto this day; because she hid the messengers, which Joshua sent to spy out Jericho" (Joshua 6:25, KJV).

Does Rahab's story resonate with any of us? Many of us carry the burden of a dark past, marked by choices and actions we now regret. However, Rahab's narrative encourages us to see beyond our mistakes and recognize the potential for transformation and redemption within each of us. As we delve into her life, let us reflect on our own journeys and acknowledge the universal truth that we all have a bit of Rahab in us.

In exploring Rahab's life, we are invited to see ourselves in her story. Her past did not define her future; instead, her faith and actions opened a new path filled with purpose and grace. As we reflect on her experiences, let us be inspired to embrace our potential for change and the boundless possibilities of trusting in God's plan.

The essence of this chapter is to emphasize that no matter how dark our past may be, it is indeed past. God's love and mercy are far more significant than even our greatest mistakes. He is always ready to transform our lives and use us for His glory, just as He did with Rahab. Her story is not just a tale from ancient times; it is a living testament to the hope and renewal available to us through faith.

As we journey through this chapter, let us hold onto the profound truth that our past does not dictate our future. Like Rahab, we can rise above our former selves, embrace God's forgiveness, and step into the new life He offers. Let us be encouraged and inspired by Rahab's transformation, allowing her story to remind us of the incredible power of redemption and the unwavering love of our Heavenly Father.

In the Book of Joshua, we encounter Rahab, one of the Old Testament's most remarkable and most discussed women. Rahab provides shelter and support to Israelite spies on an intelligence-gathering mission in her hometown of Jericho. Through her actions, she demonstrates unswerving faith and allegiance to God. Rahab's faithfulness led her to become part of the family of Israel, the lineage of King David, and ultimately, Jesus Christ.

Rahab's story unfolds with the Israelite spies arriving in Jericho, a city marked for destruction. Despite the risk, Rahab hides the spies and helps them escape, expressing her belief in the God of Israel. She says, "I know that the Lord hath given you the land and that your terror is fallen upon us, and that all the inhabitants of the land faint because of you" (Joshua 2:9, KJV). Her words reveal a deep conviction and recognition of God's power.

This act of courage and faith sets Rahab apart. She trusts in the God of Israel, defying her past and her people's beliefs. By doing so, she secures her and her family's safety. The spies promise her, "And it shall be, when the Lord hath given us the land, that we will deal kindly and truly with thee" (Joshua 2:14, KJV). Rahab's actions show that faith in God transcends one's history and circumstances.

As noted in the Gospel of Matthew, Rahab's inclusion in the genealogy of Jesus Christ underscores the transformative power of faith and redemption. "And Salmon begat Booz of Rachab; and Booz begat Obed of Ruth; and Obed begat Jesse; And Jesse begat David the king; and David the king begat Solomon of her that had been the wife of Urias" (Matthew 1:5-6, KJV). Her journey from sin to a pivotal role in salvation history is a testament to God's grace.

Her story invites us to reflect on our own lives. Like Rahab, we all have moments we regret, actions that haunt us. Yet, Rahab's life teaches us that our past does not define us. Instead, our faith and actions in the present can shape a new future. We, too, can find redemption and purpose through our unremitting faith in God.

Let us take inspiration from Rahab's transformation. Her faith led her from the shadows of her past into the light of God's promise. In the same way, our faith can guide us through our darkest moments, bringing us into a future filled with hope and divine purpose. The scripture assures us, "Therefore if any man be in Christ, he is a new creature: old things are passed away; behold, all things are become new" (2 Corinthians 5:17, KJV).

As we continue this journey, let Rahab's story remind us that God's grace is sufficient to transform our lives no matter where we come from or what we've done. We can rise above our past, embrace God's forgiveness, and step into the new life He offers. Let Rahab's legacy inspire us to live with faith and courage, trusting in God's plan and His ability to use us for His glory.

This chapter encourages us to leave our past behind and embrace the future God has in store for us. Rahab's life is a beacon of hope, demonstrating that we can overcome our darkest days and become part of God's grand narrative with faith. Let us hold fast to this truth and allow it to guide us as we move forward, knowing that a dark past is indeed past and a bright future awaits.

Examining Rahab's life offers insight into God's approach to dealing with individual believers through His grace and mercy. Rahab understood that only God could save her and her family. She fiercely protected her loved ones, showing that her devotion to God was inseparable from her care for those she cherished.

Rahab's story is undeniably complex, yet it highlights the strength and resilience that come from faith. Despite her past, Rahab stood firm and unmovable in the face of danger, demonstrating a steadfast commitment to God. Her actions during the fall of Jericho are a testament to the power of faith and the protection God offers to those who trust Him.

The Bible says, "By faith the harlot Rahab perished not with them that believed not, when she had received the spies with peace" (Hebrews 11:31, KJV). This verse underscores Rahab's faith, which set her apart and saved her from the destruction that befell those who did not believe. Her story teaches us that faith, even in the most challenging circumstances, can lead to deliverance and blessing.

Rahab's devotion to her family and willingness to risk everything for their safety and God's will reveal a heart transformed by divine grace. She believed in God's promises and acted courageously, knowing that her past did not disqualify her from receiving God's mercy. The transformation in Rahab's life is a powerful reminder that God looks at the heart and faith, not our past mistakes.

As we reflect on Rahab's life, let us consider how God's grace and mercy have worked in our lives. Just as Rahab found favor with God despite her past, we too can experience His forgiveness and redemption. "For I will be merciful to their unrighteousness, and their sins and their iniquities will I remember no more" (Hebrews 8:12, KJV). This promise reassures us that God's grace covers all our transgressions, offering us a fresh start.

Rahab's courage to stand firm in her faith, protect her family, and align herself with God's people inspires us all. Her life illustrates that no matter how messy our story, God can use us for His purposes. Rahab's inclusion in the lineage of Jesus Christ reminds us that our past does not determine our future; our faith and God's grace do.

In conclusion, Rahab's journey from a dark past to a life of faith and purpose exemplifies the transformative power of God's grace. Her story encourages us to stand strong in our faith, protect those we love, and trust in God's plan. Let us be inspired by Rahab's example, knowing that God can redeem any past and use us mightily for His glory. As we move forward, let us embrace the truth that a dark past is indeed past, and a bright future, filled with God's grace and mercy, awaits.

Rahab lived a rough life—haven't we all done things we're not proud of? None of us are perfect. Rahab's faith enabled her to turn away from her lifestyle as a harlot, her culture, and her past. She had the kind of faith that brought about genuine change; Rahab put her faith into action. She trusted God enough to move forward confidently, knowing He always keeps His promises.

God saw Rahab's faith manifested through her obedience, and He saved her. She dared to act. The Bible tells us, "For as the body without the spirit is dead, so faith without works is dead also" (James 2:26, KJV). Rahab's actions exemplified this truth. Her faith was a belief in her heart and a force that guided her decisions and actions.

Reflecting on Rahab's life invites us to consider our own. What does God see when He observes us? Does He witness our faithfulness to Him, or is our faith lying dormant? This question challenges us to examine our lives honestly. The scripture encourages us, "Examine yourselves, whether ye be in the faith; prove your selves" (2 Corinthians 13:5, KJV).

Rahab's story also highlights the importance of obedience to God. Her willingness to act on her faith, even at great personal risk, brought her salvation and a new future. The same holds true for us. Obedience to God's word and His will is a critical aspect of our faith journey. As Jesus said, "If ye love me, keep my commandments" (John 14:15, KJV). Our love for God should reflect our actions and willingness to follow His guidance.

Rahab's transformation from sin to a life of purpose is a testament to the power of faith and obedience. It shows that no matter our past, we can be redeemed and used for God's glory. As mentioned in the Gospel of Matthew, her inclusion in the lineage of Jesus Christ reminds us that our past does not disqualify us from God's plan. Instead, our faith and obedience can lead to a future filled with divine purpose and blessing.

As we continue this chapter, let Rahab's story inspire us to examine our faith and obedience to God. Are we living out our faith through our actions? Are we obeying God's commandments and trusting in His promises? Rahab's courage to act on her faith challenges us to do the same.

Let us strive to be like Rahab, whose faith was not merely a belief but a guiding force in her life. Let us have the courage to act on our faith, trust God's promises, and obey His commandments. In doing so, we can experience the transformative power of God's grace and step into the glorious future He has prepared for us.

As we move forward, let us embrace the truth that a dark past is indeed past, and a bright future, filled with God's grace and mercy, awaits. Rahab's story encourages us to live out our faith boldly, act with courage, and trust in God's unfailing promises.

Once we come to Jesus Christ and accept Him as our Lord and Savior, our past no longer matters. Humanity clings to and reminds us of our past mistakes. With Jesus Christ, our slate is wiped clean. As illustrated in Rahab's life, this is an inspiring story of how all sinners saved by grace through faith can indeed be used mightily by God.

Our past does not in any way limit God's purpose for our lives. Read that again. Rahab's transformation is a testament to this truth. Despite her previous life as a harlot, her faith and obedience opened the door to God's grace and redemption. Her story encourages us to let go of our past and embrace the future God has for us.

The Bible reminds us, "Therefore if any man be in Christ, he is a new creature: old things are passed away; behold, all things are become new" (2 Corinthians 5:17, KJV). This promise assures us that our past does not define our

future. When we come to Christ, we are made new, and our old sins are forgiven and forgotten by God.
Rahab's inclusion in Jesus Christ's lineage is a powerful reminder that God can use anyone, regardless of their past. " Her legacy is a testament to the fact that faith and obedience can lead to a life of purpose and blessing.

When we accept Jesus Christ, our mistakes are erased, and we are given a new beginning. Rahab's story teaches us that no sin is too great for God's forgiveness. God's grace is sufficient to cover all our transgressions. "For by grace are ye saved through faith; and that not of yourselves: it is the gift of God" (Ephesians 2:8, KJV). This grace is available to all who believe and trust in Him.

As we reflect on Rahab's life, remember that our past does not hinder God's plans for us. He can use our experiences, both good and bad, to shape us into vessels for His glory. Our faith and obedience to God can transform our lives, just as they did for Rahab.

Rahab's story shines as a beacon of hope for all burdened by their past. It shows us that we can overcome our past through faith in Jesus Christ and step into the new life He offers. Let us be encouraged by Rahab's example and trust that God's grace is sufficient for us.

Rahab's journey from sin to a life of faith and purpose displays for all to see the transformative power of God's grace. Her story encourages us to let go of our past, embrace our new identity in Christ, and trust in God's promises. As we move forward, remember that our past does not limit God's purpose for our lives. With faith and obedience, we can experience the fullness of God's grace and walk confidently into the future that He has prepared for us.

Rahab needed deliverance from a life of hopelessness, and she trusted God. In return, she was delivered. Her new life stands as a powerfully testifies to the world that God forgives. Who is man to judge and say otherwise?

Rahab's transformation clearly illustrates the power of faith and redemption. By trusting in God's promises, she moved from a life of despair to one of hope and purpose. Her story reminds us that no matter how far we have strayed, God's forgiveness is always available to those who seek it.

The Bible says, "If we confess our sins, he is faithful and just to forgive us our sins, and to cleanse us from all unrighteousness" (1 John 1:9, KJV). This verse reassures us that God's forgiveness is readily available and guaranteed for those who repent. Rahab's life is a living example of this truth.

Rahab's past did not define her future. Instead, her faith and God's grace transformed her into a woman of great testimony. Her story challenges us to let go of our judgments and embrace God's forgiveness. Jesus said, "Judge not, that ye be not judged. For with what judgment ye judge, ye shall be judged: and with what measure ye mete, it shall be measured to you again" (Matthew 7:1-2, KJV). This teaching reminds us to focus on our faith and leave judgment to God.

As we reflect on Rahab's journey, let us consider the areas where we need God's deliverance. Are we holding onto past mistakes or feeling unworthy of forgiveness? Rahab's story encourages us to trust in God's mercy and believe in His power to transform our lives.

In times of doubt, let us remember the words of the psalmist: "The Lord is nigh unto them that are of a broken heart; and saveth such as be of a contrite spirit" (Psalm 34:18, KJV). God is always close to those who seek Him with a humble and repentant heart.

Rahab's new life reflects God's plans for us, which are always filled with hope and purpose. Her faith led to her deliverance, and her story inspires believers to trust God's promises. As we progress in our faith journeys, let us hold onto the truth that God's forgiveness is always within reach.

Rahab's story teaches us that God's forgiveness and deliverance are available to us no matter how hopeless our situation may seem. Her life is a powerful reminder that faith can lead to transformation and that God's grace is sufficient for all our needs. Let us be inspired by Rahab's testimony and trust in God's ability to redeem and renew our lives.

God uses the most unlikely people, the most broken souls, for His glory and to advance His purposes. Who knows that we have come to our royal position for such a time as this? In God's hands, our lives have meaning. God created every individual and knew us before placing us in our mother's womb.

Rahab's story reminds us that God can transform anyone's life, no matter their past. Her journey from sin to a life of faith and purpose exemplifies God's ability to redeem and restore. The Bible states, "Before I formed thee in the belly I knew thee; and before thou camest forth out of the womb I sanctified thee, and I ordained thee a prophet unto the nations" (Jeremiah 1:5, KJV). This verse underscores that

God's knowledge and plans for us extend beyond our understanding.

God often chooses the most unexpected individuals to fulfill His plans. Rahab, a harlot, became a crucial part of His divine plan. Similarly, God sees potential in us, regardless of our past. The Apostle Paul writes, "But God hath chosen the foolish things of the world to confound the wise; and God hath chosen the weak things of the world to confound the things which are mighty" (1 Corinthians 1:27, KJV). This passage highlights that God's criteria for selection differ vastly from our human standards.

Our past mistakes and brokenness do not at all disqualify us from being used by God. Instead, they often become the elements He uses to display His glory and power. Rahab's story clearly exemplifies this truth. Her faith and actions, despite her background, led to her inclusion in the lineage of Jesus Christ. This illustrates that God's grace can turn any life around.

We are reminded of Esther's story, where Mordecai tells her, "And who knoweth whether thou art come to the kingdom for such a time as this?" (Esther 4:14, KJV). This encourages us to consider that our unique circumstances and positions are part of God's plan. In His hands, our lives are filled with purpose and meaning.

Reflecting on these biblical narratives, God's plans are intricate and purposeful. He knew us before birth and designed our lives with specific intentions. As the psalmist declares, "For thou hast possessed my reins: thou hast covered me in my mother's womb. I will praise thee; for I am fearfully and wonderfully made: marvellous are thy works; and that my soul knoweth right well" (Psalm

139:13-14, KJV). This affirms that each of us is uniquely created for God's glory.

Rahab's story and those of others like Esther's show us that God uses unlikely people to fulfill His divine purposes. No matter how broken or flawed, our lives have meaning in God's hands. As we trust in His plans and embrace our roles, we can experience the fullness of His grace and the power of His redemption. Let us be encouraged to live out our faith boldly, knowing that God can use us mightily for His glory.

Chronicles tells us, "For the eyes of the Lord run to and fro throughout the whole earth, to show himself strong in the behalf of them whose heart is perfect toward him" (2 Chronicles 16:9, KJV). God is not bound to our past, as we often are; He desires to use us despite our past and our failures. God lifts us up and strengthens us after our falls. He teaches and nurtures us.

Rahab experienced a transformation by relying on the Lord. God was new to her, yet she trusted Him. Transformation often happens through action that reveals and develops faith, not just passive belief. Our faith in action can transform us, but we have to move.

Rahab's story illustrates this principle vividly. Her decision to hide the Israelite spies was not a passive belief but a bold action rooted in faith. This courage and trust in God led to her deliverance and the preservation of her family. The Bible emphasizes, "Even so faith, if it hath not works, is dead, being alone" (James 2:17, KJV). Rahab's faith was alive, demonstrated through her deeds.

God's willingness to use us despite our flaws and failures is a recurring theme in Scripture. The apostle Paul reminds us, "And he said unto me, My grace is sufficient for thee: for my strength is made perfect in weakness" (2 Corinthians 12:9, KJV). Our weaknesses do not disqualify us from God's service; to the contrary, they allow His strength to shine through us.

As we reflect on Rahab's transformation, we see the importance of active faith. It is through our actions, inspired by faith that we experience growth and change. Rahab's trust in a God she had just learned is a powerful reminder that faith is not about the length of our relationship with God but the depth of our trust in Him.

God seeks hearts fully committed to Him, ready to act on their faith. This commitment transforms us and aligns our lives with His purposes. The psalmist declares, "Wait on the Lord: be of good courage, and he shall strengthen thine heart: wait, I say, on the Lord" (Psalm 27:14, KJV). Our courage and willingness to act, even when unsure, invite God's strength into our lives.

Rahab's story encourages us to embrace active faith. Our past does not limit God but is ready to use us in mighty ways. Our transformation comes through trusting Him and taking bold steps of faith. As we move forward, remember that God strengthens and nurtures us, teaching us through our actions and experiences. By committing our hearts fully to Him, we can witness His transformative power in our lives and fulfill the purposes He has set before us.

Whatever our perspective on Rahab, it is clear that God blessed and transformed her despite her imperfections and mistakes. Rahab was a woman of her word, and God honored that. Her life was completely changed.

Rahab's story is a powerful reminder that God sees beyond our flaws and failures. He looks at our hearts and our willingness to trust and obey Him. The Bible teaches, "The Lord seeth not as man seeth; for man looketh on the outward appearance, but the Lord looketh on the heart" (1 Samuel 16:7, KJV). This verse reassures us that God's judgment is not based on our past but on our faith and commitment to Him.

Rahab's faith was demonstrated through her actions. She made a promise to the Israelite spies and kept it, even at great personal risk. God honored her integrity and faithfulness. Her story illustrates that when we honor our commitments and trust in God, He rewards our faith. As the scripture says, "Commit thy way unto the Lord; trust also in him; and he shall bring it to pass" (Psalm 37:5, KJV).

The transformation in Rahab's life was remarkable. From a harlot in Jericho, she became a respected member of the Israelite community and an ancestor of Jesus Christ. This radical change highlights the power of God's grace to redeem and restore. It shows us that no one is beyond the reach of God's transforming power. "Therefore if any man be in Christ, he is a new creature: old things are passed away; behold, all things are become new" (2 Corinthians 5:17, KJV).

Reflecting on Rahab's journey, we see the importance of faithfulness and integrity. Her story encourages us to always remain steadfast in our commitments and trust in God's promises. It also reminds us that our past does not determine our future. God can use our lives for His glory, no matter where we come from or what we have done.

Rahab's life is a testament to the fact that God can take anyone, regardless of their past, and use them for His divine purposes. Her faith and actions opened the door to a new life filled with purpose and blessing. This teaches us that our transformation begins with a step of faith and a commitment to follow God's will.

Rahab's story offers us an inspiring example of God's grace and redemption. Despite her imperfections, she was transformed and blessed by God. Her faith and integrity were honored, leading to a complete change in her life. As we reflect on her journey, let us be encouraged to trust in God's transformative power and commit our lives to Him. By doing so, we can experience the fullness of His blessings and the joy of being used for His glory.

The story of Rahab teaches us to have empathy. Empathy is the ability to understand and share the feelings of another. It calls us to have compassion and not pass judgment on people with messy lives. May we have empathy and compassion for "the Rahabs of Jericho" because we were once in similar situations ourselves. It is not our place to determine if God is working in someone's life. Before Rahab's life changed, she had to learn who God was, and while the rest of Jericho waited in fear, Rahab took her first step of faith.

Rahab's life shines a spotlight on the importance of compassion. Have we ever stopped to consider what life must have been like for Rahab after Jericho fell? Her neighbors were dead, her life was forever changed, and she emerged from the wreckage of her city with her life, her family, and unwavering faith. Rahab had to start from scratch, demonstrating great strength and resilience. It takes immense courage to begin anew.

If we profess to love people and have a heart for God, we must stop and wonder what some poor soul might be going through, especially those who face quick judgment from others. Do we consider that their circumstances could easily be ours if the tables were turned? It could be our son or daughter in need of compassion and deliverance.

The Bible calls us to show love and compassion to others. "Judge not, and ye shall not be judged: condemn not, and ye shall not be condemned: forgive, and ye shall be forgiven" (Luke 6:37, KJV). This scripture reminds us that our role is not to judge but to extend grace and understanding, just as God has shown us.

Rahab's story also teaches us the power of faith. Despite her past, she trusted in God and took bold actions that changed her destiny. "By faith the harlot Rahab perished not with them that believed not, when she had received the spies with peace" (Hebrews 11:31, KJV). Her faith set her apart and led to her inclusion in the lineage of Jesus Christ.

As we reflect on Rahab's journey, let us be inspired to show empathy and compassion to those around us. Let us remember that everyone has a story, and it is not our place to judge. Instead, we should offer support and kindness, recognizing that God is at work in every life.

Rahab's story is a powerful lesson in empathy, compassion, and faith. Her transformation from a life of sin to one of purpose and blessing demonstrates that God's grace is available to all. As we move forward, let us commit to understanding and sharing the feelings of others, showing compassion without judgment, and trusting in God's ability to transform lives. By doing so, we can honor God and reflect His love to a world in need of grace and redemption.

It is crucial that we teach compassion, love, and understanding to our children. When someone takes that first step of faith, we should fan their flame, cheer them on, nurture their growth, and help them to grow. God help us! Do not make their past a stumbling block. Instead, celebrate God's mercy, grace, and redemption.

Our response to new believers should mirror the support and encouragement that Rahab received. By nurturing their faith and guiding them, we help them to grow strong in their relationship with God. The Bible reminds us, "Bear ye one another's burdens, and so fulfill the law of Christ" (Galatians 6:2, KJV). This verse emphasizes our responsibility to support and uplift each other, especially those who are new in their faith journey.

Rahab's story teaches us to stand strong in our faith and be witnesses of God's transformative power. Her courage and faithfulness serve as a powerful example of God's ability to redeem and restore. As the Apostle Paul wrote, "Wherefore seeing we also are compassed about with so great a cloud of witnesses, let us lay aside every weight, and the sin which doth so easily beset us, and let us run with patience the race that is set before us" (Hebrews 12:1, KJV). We are called to be examples of faith and perseverance to those around us.

Celebrating God's mercy, grace, and redemption means recognizing the potential for change in every individual. It means seeing beyond their past and focusing on the new creation they become in Christ. "Therefore if any man be in Christ, he is a new creature: old things are passed away; behold, all things are become new" (2 Corinthians 5:17, KJV). This transformation is something to be celebrated and encouraged.

In teaching our children compassion, love, and understanding, we prepare the next generation to carry forward the loving message of God's grace. Our actions and attitudes can inspire them to be compassionate and supportive of others. "Train up a child in the way he should go: and when he is old, he will not depart from it" (Proverbs 22:6, KJV). By instilling these values, we ensure that the legacy of faith and compassion continues.

As we reflect on Rahab's journey and the lessons it teaches, let us commit to being strong in our faith and a powerful example of God's love. Let us cheer on those who are taking their first steps in faith and help them grow. By doing so, we fulfill our calling to be witnesses of God's transformative power.

In conclusion, Rahab's story is a powerful reminder of the importance of compassion, encouragement, and faith. Her transformation from a life of sin to one of purpose and blessing demonstrates the limitless reach of God's grace. As we move forward, let us commit to nurturing the faith of others, celebrating God's mercy and grace, and being strong witnesses of His love and redemption. By doing so, we can inspire others and reflect God's love to a world desperately in need of hope and transformation.

Be blessed in the Lord, always!

CHAPTER 10

VESSEL OF HONOR

LET GOD USE YOU

"If a man therefore purge himself from these, he shall be a vessel unto honour, sanctified, and meet for the master's use, and prepared unto every good work."(2 Timothy 2:21)

THIS MESSAGE IS FOR those who profess to love God and harbor His love in their hearts. "I thank You, Holy Spirit, for Your Word daily!"

As we reflect on the numerous experiences that have shaped our lives, we see how each has meticulously prepared us for our journey to serve God in a significant and anointed capacity. Every trial, joy, and lesson has been used by God as a steppingstone, molding us to reach those in need or despair. Our calling may sometimes be as simple as offering a few kind words or a gesture of kindness—anything that demonstrates the love of God toward another person is invaluable. This love extends to everyone: family, friends, and even adversaries.

God's Word instructs us to love our enemies: "But I say unto you, Love your enemies, bless them that curse you, do good to them that hate you, and pray for them which despitefully use you, and persecute you" (Matthew 5:44, KJV). It takes tremendous humility to serve those who have wronged us, to extend kindness to those who have tarnished our reputation. However, the love of God always prevails. This Divine love empowers us to rise above our hurts and offenses, transforming us into vessels of honor, fit for the Master's use.

"If a man therefore purge himself from these, he shall be a vessel unto honour, sanctified, and meet for the master's use, and prepared unto every good work" (2 Timothy 2:21, KJV). Our ability to serve in this way is not born of our strength but of the Holy Spirit working within us, shaping us into instruments of His peace and love. Becoming a vessel of honor involves purging ourselves of all that is not of God, embracing His refining fire that sanctifies and prepares us for every good work.

In our service, we touch lives in ways we may never fully understand. A simple act of kindness can be a lifeline to someone in despair, and a word of encouragement can ignite hope in a weary soul. When we allow God's love to flow through us, we become conduits of His grace and mercy, reflecting His benevolent heart to a broken world. Our actions, however small they may seem, carry the potential to transform lives and draw others closer to God.

Let us embrace this calling with humility and gratitude, recognizing that every experience has equipped us for this very purpose. As vessels of honor, we are called to make a difference, to shine the light of God's love in the darkest places, and to be His hands and feet to those around us. This high calling is both a privilege and a responsibility that we must take seriously, always striving to reflect God's love and grace.

May we continually seek the Holy Spirit's guidance, allowing Him to lead us in showing love to all, regardless of their actions toward us. In doing so, we fulfill the greatest commandments: to love God with all our heart, soul, and mind, and to love our neighbors as ourselves (Matthew 22:37-39, KJV). This love is the cornerstone of our faith and the foundation of our service.

Let us strive to be vessels of honor, prepared and willing to be used by God in whatever capacity He chooses. Through our obedience and love, we can impact lives, bring hope to the hopeless, and demonstrate the transformative power of God's love. As we serve, let us remember that it is not by our might or power but by the Spirit of the Lord that we can fulfill this high calling. "Not by might, nor by power, but by my spirit, saith the Lord of hosts" (Zechariah 4:6, KJV).

We are the hands and feet of Jesus here in His kingdom. We are His tools and instruments, set in motion to do good by our fellow man, to perform selfless acts of great kindness, all to glorify His holy name. We must allow the love of God to pour through us, touching other people's lives and never passing by or ignoring a man or woman in need. "And let us not be weary in well doing: for in due season we shall reap, if we faint not" (Galatians 6:9, KJV).

Every encounter, every moment of service, is a Divine appointment orchestrated by God.

When we cross paths with others, there is no such thing as a coincidence. God orchestrates these Divine appointments for us to extend our hands, with Him working through us to accomplish His work and will. "For we are labourers together with God" (1 Corinthians 3:9, KJV). Hallelujah! Let us be ever ready to serve, love, and be the vessels through which God's purposes are fulfilled.

Some people are wonderfully anointed to help others—physically, spiritually, or emotionally—sometimes in every way. Through obedience to God, we develop a burden and desire to assist those who lack and have need. God's Word declares, "Whatsoever thy hand findeth to do, do it with thy might" (Ecclesiastes 9:10, KJV). As we pursue what we are called to do, may the favor of the Lord our God, who has placed that blessed calling upon us, rest upon us and establish the work of our hands.

Our anointing to serve stems from obedience and love for God. When we see someone in need and feel compelled to help, the Holy Spirit moves within us, urging us to act. This calling to serve is not about our glory but glorifying God's holy name. We become living testimonies of His grace and mercy by manifesting God's love through our actions.

Let us embrace this Divine calling with total commitment, knowing that our great or small service is significant in God's eyes. The work we do in His name, the kindness we show, and the love we extend all reflect His presence in our lives. "Inasmuch as ye have done it unto one of the least of these my brethren, ye have done it unto me" (Matthew 25:40, KJV).

May the Lord's favor be upon us as we serve, knowing He has equipped us with everything we need to fulfill our calling. Let us be diligent, compassionate, and untiring in our efforts, always seeking to honor God in all we do. May His name be glorified through our service, and may His kingdom expand.

In every act of service, word of encouragement, and gesture of kindness, let us remember that we are Jesus' hands and feet, carrying His love into a world in desperate need of hope and healing. As we allow the Holy Spirit to work through us, we become vessels of honor, fulfilling God's Divine purpose and impacting lives for His glory.

May the light of Christ shine through us to bring joy and beauty to a dark and discouraging world. "Ye are the light of the world. A city that is set on a hill cannot be hid" (Matthew 5:14, KJV). The Lord will establish our goings when we commit our efforts and submit ourselves to Him. "Commit thy works unto the Lord, and thy thoughts shall be established" (Proverbs 16:3, KJV). If we are faithful to God, He will be faithful to us. He will bless us abundantly when we move in obedience to Him.

It takes a selfless heart—not selfish, but selfless—to love as we ought. "Let nothing be done through strife or vainglory; but in lowliness of mind let each esteem other better than themselves" (Philippians 2:3, KJV). What a powerful thought: someone whose heart is full of love always has something to give. Love fuels our actions and makes us instruments of God's grace.

Let us strive to embody this selfless love, pouring it out freely as Christ did for us. As we do so, we will see God's transformative power working through us, impacting all the lives we touch. May our hearts be full of His love, ready to overflow into a world that needs His light and hope far more than most people realize.

In all we do, remember that our purpose is to glorify God and bless others. As we shine His light, may we draw others to Him, helping them to see His beauty and experience His love. "Let your light so shine before men, that they may see your good works, and glorify your Father which is in heaven" (Matthew 5:16, KJV). Amen.

Some can relate to this, but some cannot—life's scars have left many of us rough and rigid. However, our most beneficial asset is not a head full of book smarts and knowledge but a heart full of love, an ear ready to listen, and a hand ready and willing to help others. Our spiritual assets are far more critical. Utilizing our motivational gifts given and instilled by God is vital to the work He would have us complete and accomplish.

"He hath filled the hungry with good things; and the rich he hath sent empty away" (Luke 1:53, KJV). God equips us for our calling and journey, providing us with everything we need to fulfill His will. By focusing on our spiritual gifts and the love He has placed in our hearts, we can significantly impact the lives of those around us.

True wisdom comes from above and is characterized by love, compassion, and a willingness to serve. "But the wisdom from above is first pure, then peaceable, gentle, and easy to be intreated, full of mercy and good fruits, without partiality, and without hypocrisy" (James 3:17, KJV). By embracing our spiritual gifts and using them for God's glory, we become effective vessels in His hands, ready to accomplish the good works He has prepared for us.

Let us commit ourselves to using our God-given talents to serve others, be a source of love and support, and shine Christ's light in a world in dire need of hope and healing. As we do so, we will experience the joy and fulfillment that comes from living out our calling as vessels of honor, prepared for every good work. Amen.

A heart overflowing with love and compassion is a mighty source of inner strength, giving us the willpower to serve. To serve, we need only a heart full of grace and a soul generated by love. As the Scriptures say, "And above all things have fervent charity among yourselves: for charity shall cover the multitude of sins" (1 Peter 4:8, KJV). Love does not need to be perfect; it needs to be true. For God to be glorified, it must be genuine, sincere, and heartfelt. As written, "Let love be without dissimulation. Abhor that which is evil; cleave to that which is good" (Romans 12:9, KJV).

God creates special individuals to touch lives with His Divine purpose. "For we are his workmanship, created in Christ Jesus unto good works, which God hath before ordained that we should walk in them" (Ephesians 2:10, KJV). Our personalities differ, and thus, our spiritual gifts vary. "Now there are diversities of gifts, but the same Spirit. And there are differences of administrations, but the same Lord" (1 Corinthians 12:4-5, KJV).

Each of us operates uniquely, but we all play a vital role in the Kingdom. "For as we have many members in one body, and all members do not have the same office: So, we, being many, are one body in Christ, and every one member is one of another" (Romans 12:4-5, KJV). Together, we form the body of Christ, each part essential to the whole, working in unity to fulfill His Divine plan.

God seeks humble and bold instruments to honor Him throughout our life journey and fulfill His Divine will. He never uses anyone greatly until He tests them deeply. Reflect on this: sometimes, we fail these tests miserably, but we live, learn, and move on.

To be God's chosen and anointed instrument, we must be obedient, willing, and connected to Him with a clear, daily connection—not just occasionally or only on Sundays. As James 4:10 (KJV) instructs, "Humble yourselves in the sight of the Lord, and he shall lift you." Our devotion to God must be steadfast and unwavering.

We demonstrate our love for God by showing love for one another. Imagine a world filled with God's love instead of hate and evil; change begins with us. Each individual can cause a ripple effect, and those ripples are powerful. As Jesus commanded in John 13:34 (KJV), "A new commandment I give unto you, that ye love one another; as I have loved you, that ye also love one another."

By being instruments of God's love, we create a cascade of goodness that extends far beyond our immediate reach. This ripple effect can transform hearts and minds, leading to a world that mirrors the love and compassion of Christ. Let us embrace this call to be steadfast in our faith, unwavering in our passion, and relentless in our pursuit of God's will. Through humility and boldness, we honor God and become catalysts for change in His Kingdom.

No man or woman is a more vibrant instrument in the hands of the Lord than one who is thrilled to be who they are and who God wants them to be. Embracing our God-given identity with joy and confidence allows us to serve authentically and passionately.

We become potent vessels for His work when we are content and enthusiastic about our unique roles in God's plan. As Paul writes in Ephesians 2:10 (KJV), "For we are his workmanship, created in Christ Jesus unto good works, which God hath before ordained that we should walk in them." This verse reminds us that God crafts us for specific purposes, and our joy in fulfilling these purposes magnifies our effectiveness.

A person thrilled to be who they are in Christ radiates a light that draws others to God's love. Their genuine happiness and acceptance of their Divine calling inspire those around them. As it is written in Matthew 5:16 (KJV), "Let your light so shine before men, that they may see your good works, and glorify your Father which is in heaven." This light reflects personal fulfillment and shines as a beacon of God's grace and purpose.

Understanding and embracing our identity in Christ empowers us to face challenges with resilience and hope. It allows us to serve wholeheartedly, knowing we are exactly where God wants us to be. In this state of Divine contentment, we can fully utilize our gifts for the Kingdom, creating a ripple effect of positive change and spiritual growth.

The most vibrant instrument in the hands of the Lord is the person who delights in their God-given identity and purpose. This joy and acceptance make them a powerful force for good, reflecting God's love and glory in all they do. Let us strive to be such instruments, thrilled to be who we are and eager to fulfill the roles God has designed for us.

Once more, our walk with God is individualized. Each of us has a unique journey shaped by our personal experiences, strengths, and challenges. Let us pray with earnest hearts:

"God, bless the work of my hands. Help my mind stay on Thee. Strengthen and sustain my body and spirit. Continue to fill my heart with love and compassion. I pray that all those I come in contact with are blessed and feel Your anointing working through me. Dear God, help me grow, always abounding in Your work here in the Kingdom. Keep me steadfast and unmovable, never losing hope. In Jesus' mighty name, Amen."

Let this prayer be our daily invocation, guiding us to walk faithfully and purposefully. As it is written in Colossians 3:23-24 (KJV), "And whatsoever ye do, do it heartily, as to the Lord, and not unto men; Knowing that of the Lord ye shall receive the reward of the inheritance: for ye serve the Lord Christ."

In our walks, we must remember that God is with us every step of the way. Our unique paths are all part of His grand design, each contributing to the greater good of His Kingdom. Proverbs 3:5-6 (KJV) reminds us, "Trust in the Lord with all thine heart; and lean not unto thine own understanding. In all thy ways acknowledge him, and he shall direct thy paths."

May we continue to seek God's guidance and blessings, trusting He will lead us to where we need to be. Let us embrace our journeys with faith and determination, knowing we are part of a Divine purpose. As we grow with God, let us remain steadfast and unmovable, always abounding in His work.

In this journey, we find strength in prayer and community. We support one another, lifting each other up, as Paul encouraged in 1 Thessalonians 5:11 (KJV), "Wherefore comfort yourselves together, and edify one another, even as also ye do."

God help us all to remain faithful, hopeful, and fully dedicated in our commitment to His work. May our lives be a testament to His love and grace, inspiring others to seek His presence and experience the blessings of walking with Him.

Be blessed in the Lord always!

CHAPTER 11

LOVE OF THE FATHER AND THE SON

A LOVE THAT TRANSCENDS AND TRANSFORMS

"For God so loved the world, that he gave his only begotten Son, that whosoever believeth in him should not perish, but have everlasting life." (John 3:16)

OUR LIVES' TRUE STRENGTH is rooted in the unwavering love that Jesus Christ holds for us. This love is personal, passionate, and immeasurable. Jesus proclaimed, "Greater love hath no man than this, that a man lay down his life for his friends" (John 15:13, KJV). This statement speaks to the ultimate sacrifice, the pinnacle of selfless love we are called to understand and cherish. In this unparalleled love, we find our refuge, hope, and purpose.

God's demonstration of this love is unmatched. He sent His only begotten Son to die on the cross for the sins of the world—our sins. The Bible tells us, "For God so loved the world, that he gave his only begotten Son, that whosoever believeth in him should not perish, but have everlasting life" (John 3:16, KJV). This act shows the depth of His commitment and the breadth of His grace. Our salvation is not something we can earn but a gift freely given out of the boundless love of God.

Jesus came to earth fully aware of His destiny. He willingly laid down His life for us, embodying the perfect example of sacrificial love. The Scriptures affirm this truth, "Hereby perceive we the love of God, because he laid down his life for us" (1 John 3:16, KJV). Despite our unworthiness, He extended mercy and grace, offering us redemption and a pathway to eternal life. His journey to the cross was not just a historical event but a divine mission fueled by His deep love for humanity. Each step He took was for us, bearing our burdens, our sins, and our sorrows, so that we might be reconciled with God.

In understanding and accepting this love, we find our true strength and purpose. It is a love that transcends all understanding, a love that calls us to live in gratitude and reflect this divine love in our lives. The Apostle Paul writes, "And to know the love of Christ, which passeth knowledge, that ye might be filled with all the fulness of God" (Ephesians 3:19, KJV). As we delve into this chapter, let us be inspired by the magnitude of the love of the Father and the Son, as it invites us to embrace our journey of faith with renewed vigor and hope. This divine love is our cornerstone, guiding light, and the source of all we are called to be.

He knew us even then—some 2,000 years ago. He loved us even then. This timeless love, extending from eternity past to our present moment, is unfathomable and constant. Regardless of what happens in our lives, the Lord loves us with a love so immense that it transcends human understanding. As Scripture reassures us, "But God commendeth his love toward us, in that, while we were yet sinners, Christ died for us" (Romans 5:8, KJV). This divine love is not contingent on our worthiness but reflects His boundless grace.

God has a wonderful, divine plan for each of our lives. His plans are intricate, thoughtful, and designed for our ultimate good and His glory. As it is written, "For I know the thoughts that I think toward you, saith the LORD, thoughts of peace, and not of evil, to give you an expected end" (Jeremiah 29:11, KJV). He does not show partiality; He is no respecter of persons. The Bible declares, "Then Peter opened his mouth, and said, Of a truth I perceive that God is no respecter of persons" (Acts 10:34, KJV). What He does for one, He will do for another. His promises are for all who believe and seek Him earnestly.

God's Word emphasizes the inclusivity of His offer of salvation. The term "whosoever" in the Scriptures signifies that His grace is available to everyone without exception. "For whosoever shall call upon the name of the Lord shall be saved" (Romans 10:13, KJV). This covers everyone, regardless of background, status, or past. The heart of the Gospel is the truth that God so loved the whole world that He gave His only begotten Son, making salvation possible and accessible to every person. "For God so loved the world, that he gave his only begotten Son, that whosoever believeth in him should not perish, but have everlasting life" (John 3:16, KJV).

Oh, the power of that sacrifice! The sacrifice of Jesus Christ on the cross is the most powerful act of love the world has ever known. It is the foundation of our faith and the hope of our salvation. "Greater love hath no man than this, that a man lay down his life for his friends" (John

15:13, KJV). This sacrificial love empowers us to live with the utmost confidence, knowing that we are loved beyond measure and that our lives are in the hands of a loving Savior who gave His all for us.

We cannot boast about our love for God because we fail Him every single day. We can rejoice and find solace in His unfailing love for us because it never fails. As the Scripture assures us, "It is of the LORD'S mercies that we are not consumed, because his compassions fail not. They are new every morning: great is thy faithfulness" (Lamentations 3:22-23, KJV). His love remains constant and unchanging, a beacon of hope and strength in our daily lives.

We are all undeserving of this boundless love, yet He loves every individual—from the worst of the worst to the best of the best. The Bible teaches, "But God, who is rich in mercy, for his great love wherewith he loved us, even when we were dead in sins, hath quickened us together with Christ, (by grace ye are saved)" (Ephesians 2:4-5, KJV). This divine love is not based on our merits but on His grace and mercy. There is no love sweeter than the love He pours upon us every day. This love is a gift, freely given, that transforms and renews us.

Many of us have heard the phrase, "I asked Jesus, 'How much do You love me?' Jesus replied, 'This much,' stretched out His arms, and died." This poignant image encapsulates the depth of His sacrificial love. Jesus' death on the cross is the ultimate expression of His love for us. "Herein is love, not that we loved God, but that he loved us, and sent his Son to be the propitiation for our sins" (1 John 4:10, KJV). His arms, stretched wide on the cross, encompass the whole world, offering salvation to all who believe.

His love compels us to live in gratitude and humility, recognizing that we are loved despite our flaws and failures. This divine love, steadfast and unyielding, is our anchor in life's storms and our light in times of darkness. Let us continually celebrate and share this love, drawing strength from it and allowing it to guide our actions and interactions with others.

Lord, thank You for loving us just as we are. You have uniquely designed each one of us, and Your love for Your children remains steadfast and unwavering. We find comfort in Your love, mercy, and grace, knowing that Your affection for us does not change based on our differences or failings. "I will praise thee; for I am fearfully and wonderfully made: marvellous are thy works; and that my soul knoweth right well" (Psalm 139:14, KJV). This acknowledgment of Your intricate design reassures us of our worth and place in Your heart.

Thank You, Jesus, for taking our place on the cross, for breaking the chains of bondage, and for loving us even though we are guilty of sin daily. Your sacrifice on Calvary is the ultimate demonstration of love and redemption. "Who his own self bare our sins in his own body on the tree, that we, being dead to sins, should live unto righteousness: by whose stripes ye were healed" (1 Peter 2:24, KJV). You have set us free from the power of sin and death, offering us new life and hope.

You are so faithful and just to forgive when we confess and ask for forgiveness. Your promise is clear and straightforward: "If we confess our sins, he is faithful and just to forgive us our sins, and to cleanse us from all unrighteousness" (1 John 1:9, KJV). This assurance of forgiveness is a cornerstone of our faith, reminding us that no matter how often we fall short, Your grace is sufficient to lift us up and restore us.

In our daily lives, let us hold fast to the truth of Your unfailing love and the power of Your forgiveness. May we live in gratitude, continually seeking Your presence and striving to reflect Your love in all that we do. Your love, mercy, and grace are the foundation of our strength, inspiring us to live with purpose, hope, and unwavering faith.

We are not perfect, but we can be perfectly forgiven. Amen! Through the power of the sacrifice, we find redemption and renewal. Even in the midst of all we go through, we triumph over every challenge, for God has made us more than conquerors. "Nay, in all these things we are more than conquerors through him that loved us" (Romans 8:37, KJV). His demonstrated love is our glorious victory over everything.

Jesus won the victory at the cross—Hallelujah! The triumph of the cross is the cornerstone of our faith, assuring us of God's ultimate power and love. "But thanks be to God, which giveth us the victory through our Lord Jesus Christ" (1 Corinthians 15:57, KJV). This victory is not just a past event but a present reality, empowering us to face all of life's challenges with confidence and hope.

Through the sacrifice of Jesus, we are assured that no obstacle is too great, no sin too deep, and no burden too heavy. His love has conquered all. "For whatsoever is born of God overcometh the world: and this is the victory that overcometh the world, even our faith" (1 John 5:4, KJV). This victory is available to us every day, enabling us to live in the fullness of God's promises.

Let us embrace this victory, knowing that we are perfectly forgiven and deeply loved. With gratitude, let us reflect on the immense love shown to us and allow it to transform our lives. "Thanks be unto God for his unspeakable gift" (2 Corinthians 9:15, KJV). This gift of victory and forgiveness calls us to live with joy, purpose, and unbending faith, celebrating the triumph of the cross in every aspect of our lives.

Jesus loves us, and we are special to Him! Each of us is beautiful and unique, created with a distinct purpose and calling. We are not only important but also deeply cared for by Jesus. The Scriptures remind us of our worth: "I will praise thee; for I am fearfully and wonderfully made: marvellous are thy works; and that my soul knoweth right well" (Psalm 139:14, KJV). We are precious and lovely in His sight, cherished beyond measure.

When Jesus was on the cross, He looked ahead in time. He could see each of our faces—your face, my face—exactly where we are at this very moment. He knew every detail of our lives, every struggle, every triumph. His love transcends time and space, reaching into our present with the same power and compassion as it did over two thousand years ago.

He understood that His sacrifice was essential because He knew we would need Him right here, right now. "Looking unto Jesus the author and finisher of our faith; who for the joy that was set before him endured the cross, despising the shame, and is set down at the right hand of the throne of God" (Hebrews 12:2, KJV). The joy set before Him was the vision of our redemption and the fulfillment of our relationship with Him.

In every trial and every joy, Jesus is with us, His love unwavering and His presence constant. Let us find strength and encouragement in the knowledge that we are deeply loved and known by our Savior. He has called us by name, and we are His. "Fear not: for I have redeemed thee, I have called thee by thy name; thou art mine" (Isaiah 43:1, KJV).

With this assurance, let us embrace our unique purpose and calling, confident and joyful in the love and care of Jesus. We are not alone; we are treasured by the One who gave His all for us. As we journey through life, may we always remember our worth in His eyes and live out our calling with faith, hope, and love.

When we accept Jesus as our Savior, He takes us just as we are and forgives us completely. We become a new creation in Christ. The Bible tells us, "Therefore if any man be in Christ, he is a new creature: old things are passed away; behold, all things are become new" (2 Corinthians 5:17, KJV). This transformation marks the beginning of a new life, where the past is forgiven and a bright future in His grace awaits us.

As His children, we are protected, chosen, and empowered. "But ye are a chosen generation, a royal priesthood, an holy nation, a peculiar people; that ye should shew forth the praises of him who hath called you out of darkness into his marvellous light" (1 Peter 2:9, KJV). We belong to Him, and in His love, we find our true identity and purpose.

Whenever we start to lose our way, He is always right there for us to return to His unfailing love. "Let us therefore come boldly unto the throne of grace, that we may obtain mercy, and find grace to help in time of need" (Hebrews 4:16, KJV). No matter how far we've strayed from the Lord, it is always only one step back to His loving embrace. "I will never leave thee, nor forsake thee" (Hebrews 13:5, KJV).

Oh, the power of His love! It is a love that never gives up on us, a love that is patient and kind, a love that is powerful enough to transform and renew. Let us rest in this love, knowing that in Him, we are made new, protected, chosen, and empowered to live a life that reflects His glory.

Know therefore that the Lord our God is God. He is the faithful God, keeping His covenant of love to a thousand generations of those that love Him and keep His commandments. "Know therefore that the LORD thy God, he is God, the faithful God, which keepeth covenant and mercy with them that love him and keep his commandments to a thousand generations" (Deuteronomy 7:9, KJV). His faithfulness is unwavering, His promises steadfast, and His love enduring.

Jesus loves us so much that He invites us to come as we are and cast all our burdens upon Him. "Come unto me, all ye that labour and are heavy laden, and I will give you rest" (Matthew 11:28, KJV). His love is a sanctuary, a place of rest and renewal. The love of Jesus should make us all hunger and thirst for what is right and true. "Blessed are they which do hunger and thirst after righteousness: for they shall be filled" (Matthew 5:6, KJV). His love guides us towards our destiny, shaping our desires and aligning our will with His.

His love and His will give us promise. "For I know the thoughts that I think toward you, saith the LORD, thoughts of peace, and not of evil, to give you an expected end" (Jeremiah 29:11, KJV). It is a love that transforms our pain into purpose, turning trials into testimonies and struggles into strengths. His love redeems our past and gives us hope for the future. "And we know that all things work together for good to them that love God, to them who are the called according to his purpose" (Romans 8:28, KJV).

Amen! Let us embrace the truth of His love, allowing it to inspire and encourage us. In His love, we find our identity, our purpose, and our hope. We are part of His eternal covenant, a covenant sealed by His love and faithfulness. As we walk in this truth, may we be filled with His peace, driven by His purpose, and sustained by His unwavering love.

Let us close this chapter with a reflection that humbles me to tears: "I fell in love with a man who died for me! Nails did not hold Him on the cross, but His love for me did!" Oh, the power of the cross! Thank You, sweet Lord of Heaven! Hallelujah! "Oh, the blood—oh, what love!" He could have instantly called ten thousand angels to save Him, but He didn't—He chose us instead.

The love of Jesus is acutely humbling and overwhelmingly powerful. As the Scriptures remind us, "Greater love hath no man than this, that a man lay down his life for his friends" (John 15:13, KJV). This love held Him on the cross, not the nails, a love that surpasses all understanding and reaches into the depths of our hearts.

He could have chosen to avoid the agony of the cross. "Thinkest thou that I cannot now pray to my Father, and he shall presently give me more than twelve legions of angels?" (Matthew 26:53, KJV). He chose to endure the suffering for our sake, demonstrating the ultimate act of love and sacrifice. This choice underscores the magnitude of His love and the depth of His commitment to our salvation.

As we contemplate the sacrifice of Jesus, let us be moved to profound gratitude and awe. His blood, shed for us, signifies the greatest love the world has ever known. "But God commendeth his love toward us, in that, while we were yet sinners, Christ died for us" (Romans 5:8, KJV). This love calls us to live with purpose, hope, and a deep sense of gratitude.

Thank You, sweet Lord of Heaven, for Your boundless love and unending grace. Hallelujah! May we always remember the power of the cross and the love that held You there. Let this love inspire us, transform us, and guide us in all that we do.

Be blessed in the Lord, always!

CHAPTER 12

KNOW WHO YOU ARE FOLLOWING

CHRIST AND THE POWER OF HIS LEADERSHIP

"Jesus saith unto him, I am the way, the truth, and the life: no man cometh unto the Father, but by me." (John 14:6)

IN THE DEPTHS OF OUR souls, there exists a yearning for something greater than the confines of this earthly existence. This yearning finds its fulfillment in Jesus Christ, the embodiment of love, truth, and grace. As we embark on the journey of faith, we face choices that shape our destiny and define who we aspire to be. The fundamental question is: Whom do we choose to follow?

For many, the answer is clear—we choose to follow Jesus. My declaration shall forever be, "As long as I have breath, I will follow Christ!" This declaration embodies courage, conviction, and unshakable faith. However, following Jesus is more than a declaration; it is a way of life, a commitment to walk in His footsteps, emulate His love and compassion, and embrace His sacrifice.

In moments of uncertainty and adversity, we echo the prayer of surrender: "Lord, if anything I attempt is not Your will, let it slip through my grasp and give me peace." This prayer signifies our faith, relinquishing control and trusting in God's sovereignty. Knowing who we follow—choosing Jesus as our guide and Lord—transforms us. We discover the power of faith, the strength in surrender, and the boundless grace accompanying those who walk in the Savior's footsteps.

Amidst the cacophony of competing voices and divergent paths, the quest for steady guidance becomes a necessity. In this tumultuous landscape, one name stands out: Jesus Christ. This resounding declaration, to follow Jesus, encapsulates the resolve of those who walk in the Savior's footsteps. It is more than a statement of faith; it is a binding commitment to embrace righteousness, come what may.

The plea, "Lord, if anything I attempt is not Your will, let it slip through my grasp and give me peace," embodies surrender. It acknowledges human limitations before Divine providence, recognizing that true strength lies in yielding to higher wisdom. In a world enamored with the illusion of control, the call to "let it go" resonates, inviting us to trust in God's goodness and sovereignty.

To follow Jesus is not merely to emulate His actions but to embody His teachings, walk in His love, and extend His grace. It is a transformative journey leading to communion with the source of all existence. Guided by Scripture, inspired by saints and sages, and emboldened by Divine companionship, we find that life's true measure lies in our relationship with the One who calls us by name.

There are moments when life unravels, leaving us questioning the purpose behind the unraveling. Yet, amid uncertainty, there is unwavering assurance: God's hand orchestrates events according to His Divine plan. Losses and bewilderments often precede greater unveilings. Every closed door leads to unforeseen pathways, and every loss is replaced with immeasurable blessings. Though we may not grasp His ways, we find solace in knowing His wisdom far surpasses our understanding.

Surrendering to God's will requires relinquishing self, releasing desires and plans, and trusting His sovereignty. This journey, whether triumphant or trying, calls us to trust in God's goodness and wisdom. Despite the twists and turns, we rest assured that God is ever-present, guiding us with His boundless love.

In the intricate design of our lives, every event, challenge, and blessing are carefully woven by the Divine hand. Despite our plans, unforeseen circumstances often arise. Yet, God's involvement in our lives offers reassurance. Trials serve as catalysts for growth, strengthening faith and deepening reliance on God. What appear as insurmountable obstacles are in fact hidden opportunities for redemption and restoration.

As we navigate life's journey, may we trust that God's plans are infinitely greater. With His favor, we face a brighter future, guided by His ever-present love. Our power to alter our journey lies in our choices. However, surrendering to the Divine will brings boundless blessings. True faith involves declaring favor over our lives, aligning our actions with the Divine plan, and walking in faithful obedience. In

God's perfect timing, His promises come to fruition, and no obstacle can thwart His plan.

God's love remains unshakable despite rejection or neglect. His boundless love and grace eclipse opposition, leading us triumphantly through life's trials. Trusting in His Divine timetable ensures His promises always come to fruition at just the right moment. Attempting to manipulate God's timing is futile; patiently waiting aligns us with His will and opens space for His blessings.

God honors our autonomy, leaving the decision to believe and receive His blessings up to us. Our choices and actions are ultimately accountable to God, not societal standards. Embracing faith and accepting God's gifts is a personal journey that no one else can fulfill. We must live confidently, knowing our accountability lies with God alone.

Approaching God with humility and dependency, we seek His guidance and surrender to His plan. Trusting in His wisdom and yielding to His leading brings freedom from the burden of control. God's strength, power, and grace sustain us through trials, serving as an unmovable anchor. In moments of adversity, His strength shines, offering resilience, fortitude, and courage. His grace renews our spirits, enabling us to persevere.

Letting go means accepting aspects of life beyond our control, surrendering to Divine providence. God's focus is on guiding us towards our ultimate purpose. Sometimes, He disrupts our plans to realign us with His greater purpose. Trusting in His wisdom, even when it challenges our desires, leads to a life of Divine purpose and fulfillment. Despite uncertainties, surrendering to God's plan brings joy and liberation.

Living in the past hinders progress; dwelling on mistakes serves little purpose. What matters is embracing the opportunities ahead. Victory is rooted in unwavering faith in Jesus Christ. With Christ as our cornerstone, we overcome obstacles and adversity. His victory fuels our courage and resilience, liberating us from past burdens. Focusing on the future, we trust in the certainty of victory through Christ.

Achieving complete submission to God's will is challenging but necessary. It requires a shift in mindset, releasing desires and agendas for His purpose. Submission tests our sincerity in seeking God's will, calling for wholehearted trust in His wisdom. Despite struggles, submission opens the door to boundless blessings, inner peace, and fulfillment. It transforms us, aligning our lives with His purpose.

In moments of surrender, our greatest strength emerges. "Dear Lord, I entrust You with all my heart and soul," we declare, embracing the unknown journey with sincere, devout faith. "Wherever Your leading takes me, I will follow, recognizing Your wisdom always surpasses mine. With every step, I relinquish my desires, knowing Your purposes are higher. As long as I live, I serve and follow Christ, sustained by His love and grace. Lead me, O Lord, and I will follow, assured that every step brings me closer to the abundant life You have destined for me."

Be blessed in the Lord, always!

CHAPTER 13

INSPIRE TO BE AN INSPIRATION

LIVING TO UPLIFT OTHERS

"Ye are the light of the world. A city that is set on a hill cannot be hid. Neither do men light a candle, and put it under a bushel, but on a candlestick, and it giveth light unto all that are in the house. Let your light so shine before men, that they may see your good works, and glorify your Father which is in heaven."
(Matthew 5:14-16)

IN A WORLD CRAVING AUTHENTICITY, it's crucial that we embrace genuine sincerity in our interactions. True disciples of compassion seek to uplift rather than impress or demean. Our mission is to foster an environment where encouragement flourishes and negativity dissipates.

Our words wield significant influence, possessing the power to either uplift or harm. Each utterance can empower or devastate. Thus, we must choose our words with deliberate care, recognizing their transformative impact.

However, actions often speak louder than words. Our deeds reflect our character, leaving lasting impressions on those we encounter. As we navigate life, let our actions testify to our compassion, sincerity, and faith.

In this chapter, we delve into the essence of inspiration— how to uplift others through our words, deeds, and presence. Through illuminating anecdotes and timeless wisdom, we explore how each of us can become a beacon of hope and encouragement in a world yearning for genuine connection and compassion.

Kindness is a currency that never loses value, a gift that keeps giving long after being bestowed. Its simplicity belies its impact; kind words, though brief and effortless, possess transformative power. They cost nothing yet can leave a legacy of warmth and compassion.

Proverbs teaches us that "she opens her mouth with wisdom, and the teaching of kindness is on her tongue." This timeless truth reminds us that kindness is not a fleeting gesture but a guiding principle, a bright light in a dark world.

As we journey through life, let us be mindful of the impact of our words and actions. Cultivating a spirit of kindness enriches others' lives and brings great joy to our own. In a fractured world, kindness has the power to heal, unite, and transform.

We often underestimate the remarkable influence of small gestures. A gentle touch, a warm smile, a kind word, a listening ear—each has the power to turn someone's life around. These small acts of caring can ignite hope and restore faith in humanity.

In a world where kindness is undervalued, let us be conscious of our potential to make a difference. Seize every opportunity to uplift and inspire others, to offer support and encouragement. Through these small acts, we can make a profound difference in their lives.

Kindness flows naturally when the Holy Spirit resides within us. It's a Divine light illuminating the world with Christ's boundless love and compassion. To let this light shine, we must set aside selfish desires and yield to the Spirit's guidance.

It's crucial not to let negative attitudes dim God's love within us. Strive to embody the mind of Christ, seeking renewal through prayer and Scripture. As we do, our minds transform into powerful instruments of His grace, enabling us to be unstoppable agents of good in His Kingdom.

Renewing our minds is an ongoing journey requiring daily commitment to Scripture. This not only overcomes inner darkness but also makes us beacons of hope in a world longing for healing and restoration.

Live wisely by seizing every opportunity, guided by the Holy Spirit. Cultivate gratitude, allowing thankfulness to compel us to share Jesus Christ's peace. Our deepest longing should be to inspire others, assuring them that hope is a vibrant reality in Jesus.

In a world overshadowed by doubt, our role is to be beacons of hope. Embody gratitude's transformative power, igniting hope through our words and deeds. Inspire perseverance and cling to the promise of a brighter tomorrow in Christ.

Making a difference not only impacts others but also ignites personal growth and transformation. Guided by the Holy Spirit, we can brighten others' days, offer hope, and sow seeds of kindness.

Time is precious. Use it wisely to make a meaningful difference. Every moment is an opportunity to spread love and positivity. Our legacy lies in how we make others feel. Strive to leave a legacy of love and compassion, understanding that our impact on others measures our significance.

The Bible reminds us that goodness often faces challenges. Evil lurks, ready to derail our noble intentions. Remain vigilant, mindful of the many snares laid by the enemy. With faith and truth, navigate life's treacherous terrain with courage.

In adversity, we are not defenseless. Armed with faith, we can overcome obstacles with God's protection and guidance. Be vigilant and discerning, keeping eyes fixed on the truth. With faith, fulfill our Divine calling to be beacons of hope and agents of goodness.

The heart reveals our true character. Authenticity shines in acts of humility and selflessness, echoing Jesus Christ's compassion. A genuine believer embodies these virtues, offering kindness and encouragement in a weary world.

True love is found in everyday gestures of kindness and empathy. Emulate Christ's gentle spirit, demonstrating humility and selflessness. Let our words and deeds shine as a beacon of light in a dark world.

Be blessed in the Lord, always!

CHAPTER 14

WHEN FAITH AND FEAR COLLIDE

EMBRACE GOD'S POWER IN LIFE'S CHALLENGES

"For God hath not given us the spirit of fear; but of power, and of love, and of a sound mind." (2 Timothy 1:7)

IN LIFE'S JOURNEY, A critical juncture arises where our convictions and beliefs are tested—where actions speak louder than words. This intersection, where "the rubber meets the road," distinguishes mere rhetoric from genuine commitment. At this pivotal point, the clash between faith and fear challenges us to confront our deepest convictions and assess the strength of our resolve.

This collision between faith and fear serves as a litmus test of our spiritual mettle—a crucible where our true colors emerge. Do our professed beliefs withstand adversity, or do they crumble as soon as uncertainty comes along? This moment of truth tests the authenticity of our faith and shapes our destiny.

True faith, rooted in Jesus Christ, is not a passive assertion but a dynamic force propelling us into action. It drives our decisions, fuels our courage, and catalyzes transformative change. Genuine faith transcends words; it manifests in deeds, confident in God's constant presence.

As we stand at this crossroads, let us embrace the challenge with unwavering confidence in our convictions. Fortified by God's promises, we rise to the occasion, knowing He who began a good work in us will bring it to completion. Trials refine our faith, forge our character, and shape our destiny. Let us press forward with courage, assured that when faith and fear collide, faith will stand victorious, leading us closer to God's purpose.

At this pivotal moment, our faith encounters its ultimate trial, determining its strength and resilience. In this crucible of faith, our belief transcends speculation, becoming a tangible reality. Faith springs into action, breathing life into our convictions.

True faith is dynamic and vibrant, fueled by the Holy Spirit within us. It rests on the ever-dependable reliability of God's promises, even when unseen. This conviction affirms a reality beyond our physical senses—a spiritual realm governed by God's sovereign hand.

In the arena where faith confronts doubt, we must anchor ourselves in God's unshakable truth. This call to action activates our faith through deeds of courage and conviction. Embracing challenges with trust in the Holy Spirit's power, we navigate this intersection with strength and assurance, grounded in God's faithfulness.

In our journey of growth, we often train for future challenges. Only when tested do we discover our true strength and resilience. Adversity reveals our character, refining us like gold in a furnace. Through fiery trials, our faith is purified and deepened, teaching us to trust God's promises and cling to His unchanging truth.

Tempting as it is to rely on our own strengths or seek validation from others in adversity, true faith calls us to trust in God's faithfulness above all. As the psalmist declares, "Let God be true, but every man a liar," reminding us that God's Word is the ultimate source of truth.

Facing life's trials, let us hold fast to God's assurance, drawing strength from His promises. He who began a good work in us will complete it. We emerge from testing, refined, stronger, and more resilient than ever before.

Consider this: while preparation is vital, success hinges on execution. Practicing and planning are important, but progress materializes in action. This is where effort becomes reality.

Imagine meticulously rehearsing a speech; its impact is felt when delivered with conviction. It's the effect on others, the connections we forge, and the lives we touch that matter.

As we navigate life's challenges, let's not focus solely on preparation. Embrace moments of action and engagement, recognizing genuine progress is achieved here. Courageously step forward, confident in our abilities, poised to impact positively. It's about translating intentions into meaningful action.

Genuine faith isn't passive; it's an active pursuit involving seeking God's presence, praying earnestly, and immersing ourselves in His Word. It's about living our belief daily. To nurture strong faith, we must continually fix our thoughts on heavenly things, anchoring our trust in God's unfailing love and faithfulness.

Faith also affects how we interact with others. True faith expresses through unconditional love, devoid of judgment. Seeing others through God's eyes, extending grace and compassion, and obeying God's will, even when it doesn't align with our desires, leads to even deeper faith.

Maintaining a heart of praise and worship amid trials is crucial. Expressing gratitude for God's blessings, even in adversity, strengthens our connection to Him and reinforces our faith.

Engaging in spiritual disciplines—seeking, praying, loving, obeying, and worshipping—deepens our relationship with God and fortifies our faith. No matter the challenges, our faith remains unshakable, firmly rooted in our Heavenly Father's love and promises.

To navigate life's journey with purpose and resilience, carefully curate your inner circle. Surround yourself with inspiring individuals reflecting the values you aspire to embody. Immersing yourself in such company creates a nurturing environment, fueling your aspirations and growth.

Central to our journey is the clarity of purpose and belief in its attainability. Purpose illuminates our path, infusing actions with meaning. Anchoring ourselves in this conviction unlocks our potential, propelling us toward our aspirations.

Realizing purpose requires more than just belief; it demands spiritual exploration and growth. Delve into your spiritual core, seeking communion with the Divine. Embrace the mysteries of God's presence, igniting a transformative journey of self-discovery.

Stepping beyond comfort zones is essential for growth. In discomfort, we find opportunities for learning and expansion. Embrace challenges with resilience, stretching beyond perceived capabilities, harnessing adversity's transformative power.

Cultivating a positive mindset is foundational to success and well-being. Affirm faith and empowerment, aligning your thoughts with limitless possibilities. Declare victory over adversity, welcoming the abundance of blessings.

By surrounding ourselves with inspiration, clarifying purpose, exploring spirituality, embracing discomfort, and cultivating positivity, we embark on a journey of growth and fulfillment. Each step brings us closer to realizing our Divine purpose, becoming beacons of light and hope.

For those who seek the Lord, there's assurance of lacking nothing good. This promise grounds us in unwavering faith amidst life's storms. In uncertainty, we stand secure in God's provision and grace.

To maintain this steadfastness, root yourself in faith, trusting in God's timing and plan. Cultivate a spirit of fervent prayer, seeking God's will and guidance. Through prayer, invite His presence more fully into your life, aligning your heart with His purposes.

Extend forgiveness daily, releasing self-imposed burdens hindering God's blessings. Embracing forgiveness creates space for His grace, clearing the pathway for Divine provision.

By remaining steadfast in faith, prioritizing prayer, and embracing forgiveness, we position ourselves to receive God's abundant blessings. Surrendered to His will, we trust in the miraculous workings of His grace and favor.

Certain principles assure victory in genuine, intentional faith. Trust underpins our journey, requiring unmitigated confidence in God's promises and character. It demands a radical shift from self-reliance to complete surrender to Divine wisdom.

Cultivating trust anchors us in God's Word, resounding with His faithfulness. Strength from testimonies of His provision fortifies our faith, equipping us to face challenges with trust in His sovereignty.

Trust manifests through actions and attitudes. Surrendering control and fears to God, we experience peace and assurance of His work for our good.

Trust is the cornerstone of powerful faith—a faith that moves mountains and overcomes obstacles. Trusting Him wholeheartedly, we experience the fullness of His blessings as we walk in His love.

In the journey of faith, prayer emerges as a foundational cornerstone. It's not just words but a sacred dialogue with the Creator, believing our petitions are heard and answered.

Praying with sincerity involves approaching God's throne with reverence and expectancy, acknowledging His sovereignty. Infusing prayers with faith, we trust in God's power to intervene.

Daily prayer connects us to the Divine source, grounding us in God's Word and fostering intimacy with Him. Through heartfelt prayer, we experience God's transformative presence, strengthening our faith.

Prayer is active engagement—a partnership with the Creator. It's about surrendering desires to His will, trusting in His best for us.

Praying in the Spirit transcends human understanding, tapping into the supernatural. It enables direct communication with God, accessing His wisdom and insight.

Prayer is the heartbeat of the believer, sustaining and empowering us on our faith journey. Cultivating a lifestyle of prayer opens us to God's transformative power, allowing His will to work through us.

Engaging with God's Word daily is an enriching expedition into Divine truth. It reshapes perspectives, renews spirits, and redirects paths. It invites us to delve into His timeless wisdom and promises.

Understanding God's Word involves absorbing its essence, aligning thoughts and desires with Divine purposes. The Word acts as a guide, illuminating our path and offering clarity amidst life's complexities.

Immersing ourselves in God's Word empowers us to stand firm, declaring His promises and stepping into our authority as His children. Embracing and declaring Scripture aligns us with God's will, positioning us for His blessings.

Engaging with God's Word is an invitation to encounter Him, experiencing transformation. Delving into Scripture uncovers His love, character, and grace, leading to a life of purpose and fulfillment.

Living out God's Word requires aligning our lives with His principles. True growth comes from embodying Scripture in thoughts, words, and deeds.

Applying God's Word leads to personal transformation. Through intentional application, we deepen our relationship with Him and strengthen our trust.

Living the Word involves extending love and grace, practicing forgiveness, and obeying God's will. It's where real adventure begins, witnessing His promises come to life.

As doers of the Word, we put faith into practice, transforming our lives and glorifying God.

In a world often engulfed in shadows, we are called to embody light. As Christ's disciples, we actively illuminate the world with God's love.

Scripture reminds us we are the world's light, reflecting Jesus' glory. We are commissioned to shine brightly, illuminating the path for others.

Our light reflects Christ's brilliance. As we abide in Him, His light radiates through us, dispelling darkness and revealing His truth.

Embrace this calling with humility and courage, relying on Christ's indwelling power. Radiate with love and integrity, drawing others to Jesus.

In a world besieged by turmoil, let our lives offer a ray of hope, guiding others to God's kingdom. Shine brightly, as luminaries of the world.

In the tumultuous intersection of faith and fear, miraculous transformations unfold. This dynamic crucible tests resilience and authenticity.

Here, amidst opposing forces, we witness a shift. While circumstances may remain unchanged, our response transforms. It's a journey of self-discovery, confronting fears and emerging with strength.

Confronting faith and fear demands courage—facing the unknown with conviction. It's a journey challenging us to confront vulnerabilities and accept uncertainty.

Within this crucible of transformation, we choose: succumb to fear or stand in faith. This choice shapes actions, defines character, and determines destiny.

In adversity's furnace, we discover our essence, unveiling strength and grace. This testament to humanity's spirit and faith's power reveals our growth potential.

In this sacred space, where faith and fear collide, we are reborn—emerging stronger and empowered. This significant journey reveals our capacity for growth, showcasing the limitless potential within.

Be blessed in the Lord, always!

CHAPTER 15

LIMITLESS CHARITY

UNFAILING AND BOUNDLESS GENEROSITY

"Charity suffereth long, and is kind; charity envieth not; charity vaunteth not itself, is not puffed up, Doth not behave itself unseemly, seeketh not her own, is not easily provoked, thinketh no evil; Rejoiceth not in iniquity, but rejoiceth in the truth; Beareth all things, believeth all things, hopeth all things, endureth all things."(1 Corinthians 13:4-7)

IN THE VASTNESS OF EXISTENCE, amidst life's intricate interplay of joy and sorrow, there shines a beacon of perpetual light—a beacon pulsating with the essence of boundless love. This light emanates from the heart of Jesus Christ, radiating Divine grace and compassion.

At the core of this cosmic symphony of love lies the ineffable love of Jesus Christ—a love transcending time and space, reaching into the depths of our souls with a tender embrace. Jesus, the embodiment of love incarnate, proclaimed, "Greater love hath no man than this, that a man lay down his life for his friends" (John 15:13 KJV). These words encapsulate the very essence of Divine love—sacrificial, selfless, and unconditional.

This love is personal, intricately intertwined with the fabric of our being, igniting a fervent devotion within us. It transforms the darkest corners of our existence into beacons of hope and redemption. The magnitude of this love is unveiled in the ultimate act of sacrifice—the crucifixion of Jesus Christ on Calvary. In that pivotal moment, God bestowed upon humanity the greatest gift of all—salvation, purchased with the precious blood of His beloved Son. Jesus, in His infinite love, endured the agony of the cross, bearing the weight of our sins and offering the promise of eternal life.

As we journey into the depths of limitless love, let us open our hearts to receive the boundless blessings awaiting us. Let us bask in the radiance of God's unfailing love, allowing it to permeate every aspect of our existence and guide us on the path of righteousness. And let us, in turn, become vessels of this Divine love, sharing its transformative power with all we encounter, illuminating the world with the brilliance of God's limitless love.

In the splendor of existence, amidst life's intricate patterns of joy and sorrow, there exists a love that defies human comprehension. This love, emanating from the Divine, envelops us in its endless embrace, transcending circumstances and lifting us to higher realms of understanding.

No matter the trials or storms we face, the love of the Lord remains an unwavering beacon of hope and solace. It reaches into the depths of our souls with gentle reassurance and unyielding grace. God's love knows us intimately, understanding our deepest needs and desires even before we utter a single word.

In God's Divine plan, each of us holds a cherished place, valued beyond measure. God's love extends to all, without exception or prejudice. His love flows freely to all who seek solace and redemption in His embrace.

The heart of the Gospel reveals that God, in His infinite love, sent His Son, Jesus Christ, to bear the weight of our sins and reconcile us to Himself. This sacrificial and selfless love transcends human understanding, offering forgiveness and salvation to all who believe.

As we navigate life's winding paths, let us take comfort in knowing we are held in God's hand, cherished and beloved beyond measure. Let us bask in the warmth of His love, allowing it to illuminate our darkest moments and guide us on the path of righteousness. And let us, in turn, be vessels of that same love, sharing its transformative power with all we encounter so they, too, may experience the infinite depths of God's limitless love.

There is a thread so Divine, so sublime, it transcends our very essence. It's woven with the immeasurable love of the Creator, a love that knows no boundaries or limitations.

This love humbles me to my core, for despite my imperfections, it always remains steadfast and true. While I falter daily, God's love for me never does.

In my unworthiness, I am enveloped by His love, a love without conditions or expectations. It reaches into my soul, comforting me in my darkest hours and lifting me with its gentle embrace.

There is no sweeter love or greater comfort than the love God pours out each day. It surpasses all understanding, pervading every corner of our being with warmth and light.

When doubt and fear threaten, I look to the cross, where Jesus' outstretched arms remind me of His deep love for me.

Let us bask in His love, knowing we are cherished beyond measure. And let us share that love with the world, for in its embrace, we find strength to face each day with courage and grace.

In the vast expanse of Your love, we find refuge and renewal. Your love transcends all barriers, enveloping us in its warmth and guiding us through life's challenges. We are all intricately woven by Your hands, treasured equally as Your beloved creations.

We offer our deepest gratitude, Lord, for Your unwavering love, for Your compassion that never falters, and for Your grace that sustains us in times of need. Even amidst our failures, Your love remains a beacon of hope.

We stand humbled by Your sacrifice on the cross, where You bore our sins and shattered our bondage. Your love surpasses all understanding, blessing even the most broken souls.

In Your mercy and wisdom, You extend forgiveness to all who seek it, reminding us of Your steadfastness and righteousness. With hearts overflowing with gratitude, we raise our voices in praise and thanksgiving for Your boundless love and eternal grace. Amen.

Our lives are woven with threads of imperfection. Yet, there exists a Divine thread of forgiveness binding us to our Creator. This thread transcends our flaws, offering absolution even in our darkest moments. With each stumble, we are reminded of the unyielding grace flowing from God.

In adversity, we are emboldened by the unfathomable love of our Savior. Through His sacrifice, Jesus paved the path to victory over every trial. His love, demonstrated deeply, becomes our shield against despair and our anchor in life's storms.

As we navigate existence, let us cling to the assurance we are conquerors through Him who loves us. His love propels us with unremitting faith and courage. With hearts lifted in praise, we declare our Savior's triumph: Hallelujah, for His victory is our eternal hope!

In His love, we find ourselves cherished by the Almighty. Each of us, in our uniqueness, is designed with purpose, intentional creations of Divine artistry.

In His embrace, we discover our true worth. We are not defined by past mistakes, but by the grace flowing from His heart. Through His love, we are transformed, adorned with mercy and righteousness.

When we stray, His love remains steadfast, calling us back. In His presence, we find renewal, for His love knows no bounds. With each step towards Him, we are embraced by His love, finding solace in knowing we are His beloved.

Embrace this truth: the Lord our God reigns sovereign. He is not distant, but an ever-present Father whose love knows no end. His covenant spans generations, a testament to His everlasting commitment.

In Jesus' embrace, we find refuge. He invites us, burdened and weary, to rest in His arms. His love is a force that stirs within us a hunger for righteousness.

As we immerse ourselves in His love, we are drawn to our true purpose. His love illuminates our path, leading us to His promises. In His love, our pain finds purpose, and our trials become testimonies of His faithfulness.

Let us embrace Jesus' love, allowing it to shape our lives. For in His love, we discover hope, healing, and the assurance of a brighter tomorrow.

Let me share something deeply moving: "I fell in love with a man who died for me! Nails didn't hold Him on the cross, but His love for me did!"

These words encapsulate my faith, evoking awe for the boundless love of our Savior. His love is tangible, life-changing, permeating our existence.

In our brokenness, His love offers redemption, restoration, and grace. It is the heartbeat of our faith, driving our journey of transformation.

Let us reflect on His love, allowing it to penetrate our souls and ignite gratitude and worship. For in His love, we find hope, healing, and eternal significance. Oh, what love indeed!

Be blessed in the Lord, always!

CHAPTER 16

SUCCESS IN CHARITY
THRIVING THROUGH SELFLESSNESS

> *"I have shewed you all things, how that so labouring ye ought to support the weak, and to remember the words of the Lord Jesus, how he said, It is more blessed to give than to receive."*
> *(Acts 20:35)*

IN ALL THAT HUMANITY REPRESENTS, few threads are as vibrant or intricate as the thread of love. Love, with its depth and boundless capacity, brings rich meaning and purpose to our lives.

Across ages, cultures, and continents, humanity's heartbeat resonates with the rhythm of love—a force that transcends language, defies boundaries, and unites souls in a dance of divine connection.

From the sacred Scriptures of ancient wisdom to modern communication, the message remains unchanged: "We love because He first loved us." In this divine love, we discover our true humanity, finding solace and inspiration in the boundless affection of our Creator.

As we explore love's mysteries, let us do so with open hearts and receptive spirits, ready to uncover the truth. In God's perfect love, we find the courage to face challenges and the grace to extend that love to others.

Let us journey into the depths of love's ocean, guided by the light of God's unending love, knowing that we are forever held, cherished, and transformed in His presence. Amen.

The love of God is a divine force, a sacred current flowing with purity and endless depth. It's a love beyond measure and comprehension—a boundless expanse of grace and compassion stretching to infinity.

In God's presence, we are enveloped in warmth that melts away our fears, light that banishes darkness, and peace that surpasses understanding. It's a steadfast love, and never wanes despite our imperfections and failures.

No words can capture the enormity of God's love. It's an ocean without shores, a sky without limits—a love that knows no boundaries, conditions, or end. It embraces our brokenness, lifts us in our weakness, and carries us through every trial.

God's love is an unshakable anchor in life's storms, grounding us in hope, courage, and resilience. It's a love that never gives up and never let's go—constant, unchanging, and ever-present.

Let us open our hearts to receive this boundless love, be transformed by its power, and share it with others. In God's love, we find healing, restoration, and renewal. In His light, we discover our truest selves and deepest purpose.

The pinnacle of divine love is seen in Jesus Christ's sacrifice on the cross—a narrative transcending time and resonating through the ages as the epitome of love in action.

Consider the scene: the Creator sent His only begotten Son to bear humanity's sins in His boundless love and mercy. Jesus, driven by love, endured excruciating suffering and crucifixion to offer us redemption and eternal life.

The cross is an enduring symbol of unparalleled love—a love so pure and selfless that it defies human understanding. It reaches into our brokenness, offering salvation and reconciliation with God.

The story does not end at the cross. Three days after His crucifixion, Jesus rose triumphantly, shattering death's chains and conquering the grave. His resurrection signifies ultimate victory over sin and death—a testament to divine love's power to overcome darkness.

Truly, the nails did not bind Jesus to the cross. His boundless, unwavering love held Him there, paving the way for our salvation and eternal life.

Reflecting on Jesus Christ's sacrifice reminds us of God's deep love for us. His resurrection serves as a beacon of hope, illuminating our path and inspiring us to live lives of gratitude, faith, and love. In His love, we discover our true identity and purpose.

The truth underpinning our existence is the boundless love of the Creator—a love transcending time, space, and understanding. It's a love whispering through the ages, echoing in our souls: God loves you. Yes, you.

This divine affection knows no boundaries or conditions. It remains steadfast and unwavering, even in our flaws and failures. When we stumble, His love is an unyielding beacon of hope, guiding us back to His embrace.

God's mercy flows freely, a river of grace washing away our transgressions and lifting burdens from our hearts. It's mercy that extends beyond comprehension, offering us a path to redemption and renewal.

At its heart lies Jesus Christ's sacrifice—a testament to God's love for humanity. Through His death and resurrection, we find forgiveness and the promise of eternal life.

Let us cling to God's love's certainty in doubt or despair. Let us draw strength from knowing we are cherished, held in His hand, beyond measure. Let us live as testaments to that love, showing kindness and compassion to all we encounter.

God's love endures through every trial. We find solace, joy, and life's true meaning in its sweet embrace.

In our imperfection, we are gifted by God's perfect love—a love transcending flaws, failures, and inadequacies. God's love knows no conditions; it is freely given to each of us.

Picture a mighty river flowing endlessly with life and vitality. God's love for us is constant, unwavering, and overflowing with grace. It stands firm against doubts, fears, and uncertainties, a powerful ray of hope in the darkest nights.

In life's storms, we find solace in God's steadfast love. It anchors our souls, a refuge for weary hearts. Though we may falter, His love remains, guiding us to righteousness.

What does God ask in return? Our love, devotion, and wholehearted surrender. He calls us to love Him with every fiber of our being, offering Him our deepest affection. We find life's true essence in loving Him—purpose, meaning, and fulfillment.

Heed the commandment: "Love the Lord your God with all your heart, soul, and mind." Make His love our cornerstone, the driving force behind every thought, word, and deed. May we experience unparalleled joy, peace, and blessings from knowing and being known by the One who is Love.

Each day unfolds with God's unwavering love, embracing us like an eternal hug. This divine affection finds its fullest expression in Jesus Christ, who walked among us as love incarnate. Through His sacrificial act on the cross, we witness the pinnacle of God's love—a selfless offering knowing no bounds.

God's love flows ceaselessly into our lives through the Holy Spirit, guiding, comforting, and illuminating our path with divine grace. In the subtle beauty of a sunrise, the whisper of a breeze, and the tender touch of a friend, we encounter God's boundless love.

As we open our hearts to receive this love, we are transformed, becoming vessels of light and love in a world often clouded by darkness. Enlightened by the realization that we are cherished children of God, we are called to reflect His love in all we do, illuminating the way for others.

May we bask in God's love, allowing it to permeate every aspect of our being and radiate outward. In His love, we find solace, strength, and assurance of never being alone on our faith journey.

In God's love, we find favor and a shield against adversity. His love is a constant presence in life's trials, offering solace and strength. In moments of peril, His love is our refuge.

God's love is tangible, guiding our steps and guarding our hearts. It remains faithful even when we falter, reminding us of our worth and lifting us when we stumble.

God's love is beautifully simple. It's a gift freely bestowed, an invitation to intimacy with the Divine. He calls us to reciprocate this love in our relationship with Him and others, nurturing a community bound by compassion and grace.

God's love knows no limits. It transcends time and space, reaching every corner of creation. It's inclusive, encompassing all humanity. There is no room for judgment in His love, only reconciliation and restoration.

God's love is the cornerstone of our faith, a beacon of hope in darkness, illuminating the path to eternal fellowship with the Divine. As we bask in His love, let us extend it to others, becoming vessels of His light and agents of His grace.

God's love transforms, burning away fear and doubt and illuminating the path to peace. This peace transcends chaos, found through earnest prayer and surrender to the Holy Spirit.

In God's love, hope blooms like a flower in despair. Love and peace form a foundation for faith, standing firm in life's storms.

Love is not passive; it demands action, effort, and growth. It is more than sentiment; it is a way of life, embodying scriptural virtues. Love is honest, pure, humble, and kind. It endures trials, extends mercy, and refuses bitterness.

Love is a multifaceted jewel, reflecting divine light in existence. It cares for the broken, uplifts the downtrodden, and forgives the repentant. It is vigilant, protective, and unwavering.

As recipients of God's love, may we radiate its brilliance. Embrace love, knowing it bears, believes, hopes, and endures everything. In doing so, we honor divine love and invite its transformative power.

God's love is tangible, anchoring us in life's stormy seas. When we surrender to God, we experience His love—a sanctuary amidst trials. It mends brokenness, conquers darkness, and provides security.

God's love embodies truth. In His love, we gain clarity, discerning the truths guiding existence. Through divine love, we discern right from wrong, good from evil, and find righteousness.

God's love empowers us with the Holy Spirit, infusing us with strength and wisdom to face life's challenges. In His love, we find solace, inspiration, and perpetual support.

Embrace God's love, for it guides through darkness, heals wounds, and leads to salvation. In His love, we find refuge and strength.

Our spiritual journey's vitality ties to our love for God—a reality warranting introspection. Are we thriving with God, or spiritually impoverished?

Professing love for God is easy; the test lies in consistent actions, choices, and attitudes. Do our lives reflect love, compassion, and grace, or do we falter, causing disappointment?

Understanding our love for God correlates to spiritual well-being. God's love for us is steadfast; our love for Him shows in devotion, obedience, and intimacy.

God's love transforms lives and renews spirits. Reciprocate His bountiful love with dedication, finding strength, healing, and grace in life's journey.

Be blessed in the Lord, always!

CHAPTER 17

MIRACLES

BELIEVE TO EXPERIENCE GOD'S POWER

"And these signs shall follow them that believe; In my name shall they cast out devils; they shall speak with new tongues; They shall take up serpents; and if they drink any deadly thing, it shall not hurt them; they shall lay hands on the sick, and they shall recover."
(Mark 16:17-18)

IN THE FACE OF TURBULENT times, when darkness pervades every aspect of life, the miraculous touch of our Lord Jesus Christ stands as a beacon of hope. Challenges abound, and the need for miracles is evident everywhere. Yet, God's miraculous power is not only real but accessible to those who believe.

Faith serves as the conduit through which these miracles manifest. Are we ready to embrace this truth and take the necessary steps to witness God's power in action? Often, our hesitations and doubts become self-imposed obstacles to experiencing His miraculous intervention.

Despite physical afflictions, financial crises, relational turmoil, or personal struggles, we must cling to the unwavering belief in God's sovereignty. His ability to perform miracles knows no bounds, and His love for us transcends any circumstance.

As we embark on this journey of faith, let us do so with hearts filled with expectancy and courage. Dare to believe in the miraculous, knowing that God is faithful to His promises and capable of turning the impossible into reality. For in Him, there is limitless power waiting to be unleashed, and in His love, we find the strength to endure and overcome.

Amid life's tumultuous storms and seemingly insurmountable challenges, it is imperative to anchor ourselves in the eternal truth of God's sovereignty. His presence, like a mighty fortress, offers refuge and strength to those who seek Him.

In moments when our prayers seem to echo in silence and uncertainty weighs down our spirits, we are called to a deeper well of faith. Waiting upon the Lord is not passive resignation but an active surrender—an intentional choice to trust His timing and His ways. It is in these moments of stillness that our faith is stretched and refined, like gold in the furnace. Through waiting, our patience is tempered, our character sculpted, and our communion with God enriched.

Much like a master potter molds clay upon the wheel, God shapes us through the trials we endure. He uses every season of waiting to smooth our rough edges, fashioning us into vessels fit for His purpose. Though the process may be wrought with discomfort, we find solace in knowing that His hand guides every twist and turn.

Embrace the waiting with steely resolve, knowing it is not in vain. In the waiting, we discover strength, resilience, and intimacy with our Creator. When the time is ripe, He will unveil His miraculous works in our lives, leaving us in awe of His boundless love and unfailing faithfulness.

Often, we seek solace in the Divine only when life's challenges become overwhelming. Yet, through the darkness, God's unfaltering grace beckons us to lift our eyes heavenward and find sanctuary in His boundless love. Tragedy and despair often awaken us to the reality of a higher power, one whose mercy knows no bounds and compassion no limits. Each beat of our hearts and breath we take testifies to God's providential care, guiding us through life's trials with His constant support.

In the midst of our trials, God's voice whispers to our souls, urging us to look beyond our circumstances and behold His majesty. He longs to embrace us in His arms of comfort, offering peace that transcends understanding.

Do not wait until life's storms overwhelm you before turning to Him. Heed the gentle prompting of His Spirit, even in the calm before the storm. Drawing near to God, we find strength, solace, and the assurance that we are never alone on this journey.

Hope serves as an unwavering beacon, guiding us through life's tumultuous waters. It is the steadfast belief that our miracle isn't a distant possibility but a destined reality waiting to unfold. When we cultivate expectancy for God's intervention, we have a clear path for His mighty power to manifest in miraculous ways.

Experiencing a miracle firsthand is awe-inspiring, but embodying the living testament to God's miraculous handiwork transforms us from within. In moments of eager anticipation, when our faith stretches to its limits, we draw closer to the precipice of our breakthrough. It is precisely at this juncture that adversarial forces seek to undermine our faith and cast us into doubt. The adversary understands that if we grasp our miracle, we become potent warriors in the Kingdom, armed with irrefutable evidence of God's miraculous workings.

Do not vacillate in the face of adversity, for the path to our miracle often traverses trials and tribulations. With unwavering faith and resolute determination, press forward, knowing that beyond the tempest lies the radiant dawn of our long-awaited miracle.

God's ability to transform chaos into order and turn mistakes into miracles testifies to His infinite wisdom and boundless love. Amid life's turmoil and confusion, He weaves together the threads of our existence, creating beauty and purpose. In our lowest moments, grappling with doubt and uncertainty, God's miraculous touch becomes apparent. He steps into our darkest moments, illuminating the path ahead with His Divine light and guiding us toward a brighter tomorrow. His miracles defy logic and exceed human understanding, reminding us of His limitless power and abiding presence in our lives.

In the awe-inspiring spectacle of His miraculous works, we discover that His greatest miracles often unfold within us.

Empowered by His Spirit, we become vessels of His grace, channels through which His love and compassion flow into the world. Through our willingness to surrender to His will, His miracles are brought to fruition, transforming lives and inspiring hope in the hearts of all who witness His wonders.

As we stand on the precipice of possibility, we are reminded that the same power that raised Jesus from the dead resides within us. Each step we take in faith propels us toward a future filled with promise and potential, fueled by the knowledge that God's miraculous power knows no bounds.

In the depths of our need, when every fiber of our being cries out for Divine intervention, God stands ready to respond. He doesn't just hear our pleas; He listens with a depth of compassion beyond our comprehension. With every whispered prayer and every heartfelt plea, He leans in, attuned to the rhythm of our souls.

Belief is the key that unlocks the door to God's miraculous power. It is not merely about mouthing words or going through motions; it is about anchoring our faith in the certainty of His promises. When we dare to believe and hold onto hope with unyielding tenacity, the miraculous begins to stir.

Prayer is more than a ritual; it is a sacred conversation with the Creator of the universe. It is our lifeline, our direct line to the heart of God. In prayer, we lay bare our deepest fears and wildest dreams, trusting that He hears every word, every sigh, every unspoken plea.

In our darkest moments, when the night seems endless and the dawn feels like a distant dream, we keep praying and believing. We know that in the hands of our loving Father, even the bleakest situations can be transformed into stories of redemption and restoration.

So let us pray with boldness and confidence, knowing that our God is a God of miracles. Let us hold onto hope with unwavering faith, trusting that He who promised is faithful to fulfill every word spoken over us. In the sacred space of prayer, where heaven meets earth, miracles unfold, turning our deepest needs into testimonies of His boundless grace and unfailing love.

The resolute faithfulness of God stands as an unyielding pillar, a testament to His enduring love and mercy. This truth should humble every soul, driving us to our knees in heartfelt repentance and surrender. Within His faithfulness lies our ultimate hope, redemption, and salvation.

Consider the transformative power if every heart, from rulers to the most modest individuals, bowed before the throne of grace in genuine contrition. If the Church, the radiant beacon of His light in a dark world, led the charge in turning away from sinful inclinations, imagine the profound impact on our collective existence.

It is a clarion call to radical humility and a recognition of our desperate need for Divine intervention. Only when we confront the harsh reality of our fallen nature, laying bare our weaknesses and failures before Him, do we unlock the floodgates of His mercy.

Admittedly, it may sting to confront the depths of our imperfections and grapple with the weight of our transgressions. In that poignant reckoning lies the seed of revival, the promise of renewal, and the prospect of miracles.

Let us respond to the call to repentance with hearts softened by the overwhelming grace of our Savior. Let us embody a Church that leads by example, showcasing the transformative power of God's love.

In our collective repentance, the flame of revival is ignited, setting ablaze a wildfire of redemption throughout our lives, communities, and world. As we humbly submit ourselves before Him, turning away from sinful ways, we create fertile ground for His miraculous healing to sweep through every corner of our existence.

In life's tumultuous journey, let us find solace in the unshakable promise of God's faithfulness. Despite storms and obstacles, we are called to anchor ourselves in the unshakeable truth of His Word.

Stand strong amidst turbulence, grasping firmly onto His promises. Even when shadows of doubt and fear threaten to engulf us, His light shines brightly, illuminating our way through the darkest nights.

Do not resign to the dictates of circumstances; instead, eagerly anticipate God's miraculous intervention. With hearts brimming with hope and expectancy, boldly proclaim His promises, knowing He is faithful to fulfill every word.

Though the timing and manner of our miracle may remain veiled in mystery, rest assured in the certainty of His goodness and sovereignty. Whether our breakthrough arrives now or in eternity, we can trust in His unfailing love to touch us and make us whole.

So hold fast, dear friend, and do not lose heart. In waiting, believing, and trusting, we find ourselves enveloped in the tender embrace of our Heavenly Father, who holds our lives securely in His hands. Amen and amen!

Amidst life's whirlwind of activity, God's miraculous hand is at work, weaving threads of Divine intervention into our existence. Yet, too often, these marvels pass us by unnoticed, overshadowed by routine noise and distractions.

Pause, open your eyes and heart to the subtle wonders surrounding us. Cultivate a spirit of gratitude, recognizing even the smallest gestures of grace with heartfelt praise. Doing so positions us to witness the extraordinary power of God unleashed in our lives.

In II Chronicles, we find a timeless principle: praise precedes victory. As we lift our voices in adoration, declaring His faithfulness in adversity, we pave the way for His miraculous provision to manifest.

Embrace this invitation to praise, offering our gratitude as incense before the throne of grace. Cultivate a heart attuned to the whispers of His love, ever ready to acknowledge His handiwork.

In the symphony of our praise, we unlock heaven's gates and invite His miraculous power to transform our circumstances. May this truth resonate deeply, inspiring continual thanksgiving and praise.

In life's trials, where circumstances defy human logic and solutions elude us, we encounter the boundless power of God. It is in these moments of impossibility that His love shines brightest, beckoning us to trust Him wholeheartedly.

When our resources are depleted, and efforts fall short, we must surrender control and place our faith in God's hands. He alone holds the keys to unlock the doors of possibility, to turn the tide of our circumstances with a single word.

In our deepest need, we cling to the promise of miracles, believing in the transformative power of His grace. Our hearts echo with the assurance that God is not only able but eager to intervene, making a way where there seems to be none.

He is our Miracle Worker, who parts seas and moves mountains with His breath. As we stand in awe of His majesty, we are reminded that our role in this Divine partnership is faithfulness and expectation.

While we may yearn for immediate answers, we must recognize that God operates on His own timetable, according to His perfect wisdom. Our task is to remain steadfast in love and devotion, trusting He will honor our faithfulness with His own.

Cast aside doubt and fear, and embrace a posture of expectation and trust. In the hands of our Miracle Worker, there is no problem too great, no situation too dire. As we commit ourselves to His care, we can rest assured that He will indeed make a way, fulfilling His promises in His perfect timing.

In the intricate design of life, where the mundane intertwines with the miraculous, we stand at the crossroads of action and belief. It is within this nexus that the trajectory of miracles is shaped, influenced by our response to the Divine call.

Living righteously, guided by faith and virtue, lays the groundwork for miracles. Righteousness alone is insufficient; it must be coupled with fervent prayer. Do not delay, for the urgency of our prayers may be the key to unlocking Divine intervention.

God, in His omniscience, may await our petitions before bestowing miracles upon others. Each prayer serves as a catalyst for heavenly intervention, a plea that sets in motion His miraculous workings. Thus, pray with unwavering faith, trusting in the potency of our supplications.

Along the journey of faith, moments of doubt may cloud our resolve, casting shadows upon our trust. But in these moments of darkness, God's faithfulness shines most brilliantly. He waits until the eleventh hour not to test our endurance but to reveal His boundless power and sovereignty.

In the ordinary rhythms of life, God performs extraordinary acts. He weaves the threads of our daily existence into His glory, transforming the commonplace into the miraculous. Through this process, He reminds us that every prayer is heard, every act of faith noted.

Do not grow weary or lose heart. In waiting, praying, and trusting, miracles are birthed. When they come to fruition, they will stand as monuments to the power of God, a beacon of hope for all who witness His miraculous hand at work.

In moments of deep contemplation, we understand the truth that each of us may serve as a beacon of hope, a vessel of Divine intervention in others' lives. It urges us never to overlook any opportunity to extend kindness and assistance, for we may be the answer to someone's prayers, the tangible manifestation of God's grace.

Humanity often sees God working through the hands and hearts of His people. Whether a comforting word, a healing touch, or a selfless act of service, each gesture has the potential to spark a miracle in someone else's life.

Consider dedicated healthcare professionals—doctors, nurses, and caregivers—who channel God's healing power through their expertise and compassion. Through their skills and dedication, they become conduits of Divine intervention, bringing solace and restoration to those in need.

Similarly, in our everyday interactions, we are called to emulate the hands and feet of God on earth. Guided by the prompting of the Holy Spirit, we reach out to those who are hurting, marginalized, or in need. Through these small acts of kindness and obedience, miracles are often realized.

Remain attuned to the gentle whispers of the Holy Spirit, ready to respond with compassion and generosity. By opening our hearts and extending our hands, we participate in unfolding God's miraculous work, becoming agents of His love and mercy in the world.

Repeatedly, we witness God's incredible hand at work, transforming the impossible into reality. His power knows no limits, turning the darkest moments of tragedy into triumphs of light and hope. In our deepest struggles, we find consolation in the enduring promise of His sovereignty and mercy.

God's ways are beyond our understanding, His actions beyond our comprehension. In His goodness, He extends His hand to us, offering hope and redemption in the midst of chaos and despair.

As we journey through life's complexities, hold fast to the belief that God is ever-present and faithful. He is the anchor in the storm, the guiding light in the darkness. In His presence, fear fades, doubt dissipates, and faith is fortified.

Lift your voice in praise and thanksgiving, for in God's hands, miracles abound. His love knows no bounds, His grace knows no end. Though challenges may seem insurmountable, trust in His promise to make all things possible.

In life's woven threads of hope, faith, and love, we find ourselves immersed in moments of Divine grace and wonder. Each new dawn paints a masterpiece of colors, reminding us of the miraculous beauty surrounding us.

In the whispers of the wind, the laughter of children, the blossoming of flowers, and the dance of sunlight, we encounter the fingerprints of a loving Creator. His miracles are not distant events of the past but present manifestations of His boundless love, waiting to be embraced and celebrated.

As we journey through life, let us anchor our souls in the belief that miracles are orchestrated acts of Divine intervention. With hearts open and spirits aligned with His will, we become conduits for God's signs and wonders.

Lift your voice in gratitude to the One who orchestrates these miracles, acknowledging His presence in every breath and heartbeat. In the rhythm of life and the symphony of creation, we find the promise of hope and the assurance of His steadfast love.

Be blessed in the Lord, always!

CHAPTER 18

ENUMERABLE BLESSINGS

INFUSE YOUR LIFE WITH PURPOSE

"Blessed be the God and Father of our Lord Jesus Christ, who hath blessed us with all spiritual blessings in heavenly places in Christ."(Ephesians 1:3)

Blessings are the golden threads woven by the Divine hand, whispering love and favor from eternity with endless generosity. Whether subtle or magnificent, blessings reflect Divine benevolence, infusing our lives with purpose and meaning.

Pause amidst life's chaos and take a deep breath. Each breath is a precious gift, echoing the universe's heartbeat and reminding us of the Divine presence that sustains us. We often overlook these miracles in life's hurried pace, ensnared by worldly concerns. Yet, within life's ebb and flow, a constant exists—a Divine promise transcending time and space, assuring us that the Creator's tender care cradles every breath and heartbeat.

Embarking on a journey of gratitude requires humility and reverence. Each blessing, grand or subtle, reflects our Heavenly Father's infinite love and providence. Pause and count your blessings, recognizing each as a token of Divine grace. This sacred practice transforms our souls, awakening us to the beauty and abundance surrounding us.

Bow your heads in humble appreciation for the boundless blessings from our Heavenly Father. Overflowing with gratitude, acknowledge His mercy and grace in our lives. In quiet reflection, marvel at the many blessings woven into our existence. From the breeze's caress to the morning sun's warmth, from loved ones' embrace to solitude's solace, His blessings remind us daily of His unfailing love and providence.

Even amid life's storms and challenges, stand firm in His faithfulness. He has performed great and wondrous deeds beyond comprehension, guiding us through dark valleys with unyielding strength and compassion. As we greet each new day, let our hearts resonate with joy and glory. Offer our deepest gratitude to the One who bestows blessings beyond measure, recognizing every good gift from His loving hand.

In every life season, in every triumph and trial, never cease to acknowledge His goodness and provision. In His presence, we find true abundance; in His love, we discover the greatest blessing—a life filled with purpose, peace, and everlasting hope.

In our modern lives' relentless pace, we risk overlooking life's present beauty. Each moment holds miracles waiting to be noticed—from rustling leaves to dawn's soft glow. We miss these gifts in our haste, hurrying through our days without pause.

Slowing down means embracing the present moment and savoring life's richness. It's about lingering over a cup of coffee, listening to children's laughter, or watching a sunset. In our fast-paced world, slowing down is a radical act of self-care, reclaiming our humanity.

Let us take a deep breath, slow our pace, and open our eyes to the surrounding beauty. Cultivate gratitude for the countless daily blessings. Discover life's true richness and depth in stillness—the beauty of being fully present in the miracle of life itself.

Redirect attention to the overlooked daily beauty. By slowing our pace and attuning our senses, we uncover blessings waiting to be discovered. Each day offers opportunities to marvel at nature's intricacies, human connection, and simple pleasures.

Embrace mindfulness and gratitude, cultivating awareness of daily blessings. Beauty exists in every corner, whether in the rustling leaves, a sunset's vibrant hues, or a loved one's embrace. Please slow down, breathe, and open your hearts to the wonders around us. Often, the greatest blessings come from simple joys.

We can remarkably bless our family, children, and friends through gratitude and love. Nurture thankfulness, acknowledging and cherishing each person's unique presence and affection. Express gratitude for their contributions, creating a nurturing environment where love flourishes.

Invest time in meaningful connections through kindness, empathy, and forgiveness. Listen actively, fostering trust and understanding. Embrace differences, enriching our shared journey. Commit to lifting one another in prayer, interceding for loved ones, and inviting heavenly blessings.

Embody gratitude, love, and selflessness in relationships, becoming conduits of blessing and transformation. Sowing seeds of kindness and compassion, we reap a harvest of joy, fulfillment, and abundant blessings, enriching our lives and those we hold dear.

The hymn "Count Your Blessings" resonates deeply, carrying memories of loved ones and church communities. Its lyrics hold timeless truths. Amid daily routines, we often overlook countless blessings. Reflecting reveals simple joys and abundant gifts—a sun-kissed morning, a loved one's embrace, good health, and opportunities.

Enumerating our blessings renews our perspective on God's love and care. Whether grand or modest, each blessing is a token of Divine favor. Reflecting on blessings reminds us of God's faithfulness and presence. Through life's twists and turns, He guides and provides with tender care. Cultivate a spirit of gratitude, acknowledging God's goodness and opening ourselves to more abundant blessings.

In daily life's rush, we all too easily overlook quiet miracles. Chasing goals and possessions, we miss abundant blessings. Life may not follow our plans, but within challenges lie hidden blessings. In stillness and reflection, we glimpse the Divine hand at work: Sunrise's beauty, children's laughter, a loved one's embrace—all reminders of grace.

Counting blessings, savoring each moment with gratitude, reveals true wealth in relationships, experiences, and the world's beauty. Gratitude transforms challenges into growth opportunities. Even in adversity, there is much to be thankful for. Trust that even in darkness, light guides us home.

Pause now to count blessings with open hearts and minds. Embrace each moment's gift, cherishing beauty and wonder. Counting blessings reveals life's true abundance and the boundless love sustaining us.

In life's ebb and flow, gratitude unlocks boundless blessings. Life's fleeting and fragile moments urge us to pause, reflect, and give thanks for myriad gifts. Quiet contemplation reveals life's essence—dawn's light, a loved one's embrace, children's laughter. These moments, ordinary but sacred, remind us of grace.

Those who have weathered life's storms understand gratitude's depth. Trials forge wisdom transcending time, born of experience, nurtured by resilience, and steeped in gratitude. Heed gratitude's call and appreciate life's blessings. Gratitude offers solace, strength, and joy, unlocking a life filled with abundance, purpose, and love.

In modern life's relentless rhythm, busyness ensnares us. Amid obligations and distractions, gratitude is the antidote to discontent. Blessings abound for those who choose to see. Regret traps us in what-ifs and should-haves. Each moment offers freedom from regret, embracing present richness.

Gentle breezes shared smiles, loved ones' embrace, quiet moments—blessings manifest in myriad forms, each a testament to life's beauty. Recognizing and practicing gratitude awakens us to abundance, shifting focus from lack to sufficiency.

Let us not let daily life's noise drown out blessing whispers. Pause to breathe deeply, look around, and give thanks for countless gifts. Gratitude opens us to boundless wonders, inviting peace, joy, and fulfillment into our hearts and minds.

The hymn's soulful lyrics evoke gratitude, stirring thankfulness for life's abundance. Amid trials, Divine provision and care are unwavering. Each aspect of existence reflects Divine generosity from a roof's sanctuary to a bed's warmth, from food's sustenance to shoes' protection.

Beyond tangible blessings lies the Creator's boundless love, sustaining us through trials and despair. The hymn acknowledges family—a precious treasure enriching life with love, companionship, and shared memories. Embrace family, finding strength and devotion in nurturing relationships.

Reflect on blessings, tangible and intangible. Offer thanks for Divine grace manifesting in our lives. Hearts overflow with joy and appreciation for the boundless blessings surrounding us daily.

As Thanksgiving approaches, it reminds us of gratitude, generosity, and life's blessings. It's a time for communal love and appreciation, basking in familial ties' warmth and surrounding abundance. But let gratitude extend beyond a single day. Embrace daily thankfulness, recognizing life's manifold blessings.

Daily gratitude encompasses obvious and hidden blessings, even in trials. Adversity teaches resilience and strength. Gratitude weaves joy into mundane, beauty into ordinary, and grace into challenges. Cultivate a thankful spirit, enriching our lives and uplifting others.

Commit to daily thankfulness in a spirit of thanksgiving. Count blessings, both grand and subtle, and express gratitude for existence. Sow seeds of kindness, compassion, and joy, creating a ripple effect of positivity touching lives far beyond our own.

Reflect on invaluable individuals in our lives—family, friends, mentors. These pillars of strength, beacons of light, and sources of love enrich our journey. Daily life's hustle may overshadow gratitude expressions. Don't let moments slip past without conveying deep appreciation.

Tomorrow is never guaranteed; express thanks before it's too late. Cultivate a culture of appreciation in relationships where gratitude flows freely, kindness is common, and love is celebrated. A grateful heart is a peaceful heart that recognizes life's abundant blessings.

Offer thanks to the Divine for these extraordinary individuals. Shower them with love, respect, and appreciation, ensuring they know their impact on our lives.

Be blessed in the Lord, always!

EPILOGUE

EMBRACE GRACE AND RESTORE YOUR SOUL

AS WE COME TO THE END of this journey, we stand at the threshold of a new chapter, having embraced the limitless grace of God that restores, renews, and empowers. Through these pages, we have explored the countless blessings and boundless love that are available to those who walk in faith, knowing that God's plan for us is greater than any obstacle we might face. His grace is not just a gift, but a transformative force that infuses our lives with purpose, directing our hearts and hands toward the fulfillment of His will.

In the chapters we've explored, we have learned that true restoration comes from God's loving touch, guiding us through trials, infusing us with strength, and renewing our spirits. As we reflect on *"Enumerable Blessings"* and the purpose that comes from knowing God's plans for us, we are reminded of the abundant life He promises to those who trust in Him. We are His vessels, meant not only to receive His blessings but to share them with a world in need.

Belief in God's power has been a constant theme throughout this book. As we *"Believe to Experience God's Power,"* we are reminded that His miracles are not distant occurrences but are present in our everyday lives when we trust in His ability to do the impossible. Just as faith moves mountains, so does it bring restoration and hope to hearts in need.

The encouragement to *"Embrace God's Power in Life's Trials"* has been at the heart of our journey. We know that, with God on our side, there is no trial too great and no challenge too overwhelming. The divine protection and provision He offer us are unfailing, equipping us to endure with perseverance and emerge victorious. Through His grace, we are reminded that we are never alone.

As we reflect on *"Success in Charity"* and the purpose of living a life of selfless giving, we are reminded that our blessings are not meant to be kept to ourselves but shared with others. True success in God's eyes is found not in material gain but in the depth of our love and the generosity we extend to those around us. Through charity, we reflect God's heart and experience His joy.

In these pages, we have learned that faith and fear often collide in our lives. *"When Faith and Fear Collide,"* we are reminded that fear has no place when we walk in the light of God's love. The more we lean on Him, the more His grace quiets our doubts and strengthens our resolve.

As we conclude this book, we are reminded of the truth that *"A Dark Past is Past."* Through God's forgiveness and grace, our past does not define us. His redemption has made us new, and it is His love that propels us forward into a future filled with hope and purpose.

Soul Stirrings, Inspirational Messages with Grace to Restore has been a journey of discovering the boundless blessings that are ours in Christ. Through every trial, every challenge, and every moment of doubt, we are assured that God's grace is sufficient, His love never-ending, and His purpose for our lives greater than we could ever imagine.

As you close this book, know that God's grace is forever available to you, to restore you to wholeness, empower you with purpose, and infuse you with the strength to fulfill the calling He has placed on your life. With Him, you will experience the miracle of transformation, knowing that His love and His power are always with you.

"Blessed be the God and Father of our Lord Jesus Christ, who hath blessed us with all spiritual blessings in heavenly places in Christ." (Ephesians 1:3)

"For I know the thoughts that I think toward you, saith the Lord, thoughts of peace, and not of evil, to give you an expected end." (Jeremiah 29:11)

May this message of grace and restoration continue to inspire you as you walk in His purpose, share His love, and experience His miraculous power every day of your life.

And be sure to add every book in this series to you collection and share with others.

In His service and for His glory,

Anita Hackley Lambert

About The Author

As the author of "Soul Stirrings," Anita Hackley Lambert invites readers to embark on a transformative journey of self-discovery and spiritual growth. Through this book, the author aims to uplift and empower readers to embrace their faith, trust in God's plan, and navigate life's challenges with faith, courage, and grace.

With a passion for helping others live authentically and purposefully, Ms. Lambert inspires and motivates individuals worldwide to pursue their dreams, overcome obstacles, and live meaningfully.

Anita Hackley Lambert is a dynamic spiritual leader, evangelist, author, motivational speaker, genealogist, historian, and business owner. Guided by the timeless wisdom of the Bible, she empowers individuals to live with purpose and passion, equipping them to embrace their true identity and reach their fullest potential.

As a gifted seer with divine insight, Ms. Lambert draws from her journey and biblical principles to deliver messages of hope and transformation. Her writing and speaking are enriched by what she calls "divine downloads from the Holy Spirit," inspired revelations that offer Bible-based encouragement and guidance to those on their spiritual path.

Driven by a deep desire to uplift and impact lives, Ms. Lambert shares practical wisdom messages and heartfelt insights that resonate with individuals seeking spiritual clarity and direction. Her compassionate approach and unwavering faith have touched countless hearts, helping many find purpose and strength in times of uncertainty.

As the author of "Soul Stirrings: Inspirational Messages Through Revelation," Ms. Lambert invites readers to embark on a life-changing journey of self-discovery and spiritual growth. Through her words, she inspires readers to trust in God's divine plan, embrace their faith, and navigate life's challenges with courage, grace, and unwavering trust in God.

With an enduring passion for helping others live authentically and meaningfully, Ms. Lambert motivates individuals to pursue their dreams, overcome obstacles, and walk in the fullness of their God-given potential.

OTHER BOOKS BY
ANITA HACKLEY LAMBERT

Upcoming Publication of Additional Books in my Soul Stirrings' Series

BOOK 2: Soul Stirrings, Inspirational Messages With Grace To Restore (2025)

BOOK 3: Soul Stirrings, Inspirational Messages With God On Your Side (2025

BOOK 4: Soul Stirrings, Inspirational Messages As You Go Through
(2025)

BOOK 5: Soul Stirrings, Inspirational Messages For An Extraordinary Life 2025)

BOOK 6: Soul Stirrings, Inspirational Messages For The Path Foreword, 2025)

Previously Published Historical Biographies

F.H.M. MURRAY, First Biography of a Forgotten Pioneer for Civil Justice, August (2006)

ECHOES OF A VOICE FOR JUSTICE, The Story of Barry A. Murray, February (2024)

Where to Buy My Books

Embark on a spiritual enlightenment with "Soul Stirrings: Inspirational Messages Through Revelation." Delve into a six-book collection of empowering narratives that offer insights and timeless wisdom for navigating life's challenges and triumphs. These pages hold the keys to unlocking your fullest potential, whether seeking guidance, encouragement, or a deeper connection with your inner self.

Soul Stirrings, available on Amazon.com, Barnes & Noble, and other trusted online retailers, opens the door to a journey that transcends everyday understanding—a journey of faith, introspection, and spiritual renewal. This transformative series beckons readers to explore the profound depths of the soul, cultivating a deeper and more intimate relationship with Jehovah God, the Creator. Each volume serves as a heartfelt invitation to uncover the wisdom, solace, and strength within, offering encouragement and guidance for navigating life's myriad twists and turns.

Don't let the opportunity to enrich your life and nourish your spirit pass by. Order your copy of Soul Stirrings today and enter a world of enlightenment and empowerment.

This series illuminates the pathway to inner peace and spiritual growth through uplifting narratives and timeless messages, touching the heart and reviving the spirit with every page. Allow each message to inspire, uplift, and renew your sense of purpose, making Soul Stirrings a series of books and a faithful companion in your walk of faith. Embrace the journey, and let each page be a source of unwavering strength and peace as you draw closer to God and discover the transformative power of His Word.

While you browse my books, be sure to check out my historical biographies and discover my family secrets hidden in the lives of Barry A. Murray and F.H.M. Murray.

For signature or bulk copies of this book, email the author:
aHackleylambert@gmail.com

Follow me to stay up to date on my writing at:.
AnitaHackleyLambert.com
Email: author@AnitaHackleyLambert.com
Instagram: @anitalambert023
FaceBook.com:/profile.php/?id=61552071992665

www.ingramcontent.com/pod-product-compliance
Lightning Source LLC
LaVergne TN
LVHW051038080426
835508LV00019B/1583